Also by Arnold J. Mandell, M.D.
THE NIGHTMARE SEASON

COMING

MIDDLE

OF ∧ AGE

A JOURNEY
BY
ARNOLD J. MANDELL, M.D.

SUMMIT BOOKS
NEW YORK

Library of Congress Cataloging in Publication Data

Mandell, Arnold J   date.
A journey into the second cycle of life.

1. Men—Psychology. 2. Middle age—Psycho-
logical aspects. 3. Brain. 4. Coronary heart
disease—United States—Biography. 5. Mandell,
Arnold J., 1934–
I. Title.
BF692.5.M36   616.8'9'0924 [B]   77-12393
ISBN 0-671-40008-8

COMING
MIDDLE
OF ∧ AGE

ONE

I grew up in my profession getting psychoanalyzed about killing and getting killed by my father; electrically stimulating cat brains to evoke rage and penile erections; looking in the head for the hormones of power; fighting with a woman for twenty-two years about the biological bases of sex roles; driven to become a chairman of a university department; feeling constantly on trial to prove my strength; haunted by the shadows of young geniuses ready to come out of the bushes to take my job; demanding that my two boys learn to stand up and fight, especially me. I watched male baboons dominate their females. Were those red-seated, cowering ladies willing because the little but ferocious male would take on the next pride of lions?

I'm a refugee from the gonadal thoughts of Charles Darwin. He wrote the basic code for all the behavioral sciences: from ethology to neurobiology. Growing up, fighting for territory, mating, feeding and protecting children, and the attendant social arrangements were the brain's truth. In man, it's all in the first thirty-five years. Grades in "getting along with others" derive from the starvation or assault by wild animals that came with being put out of the tribe. Nowadays the diagnosis of mental illness, both major and minor, comes from the quality and quantity of interpersonal relationships.

When you're through having children, or, as is hap-

7

pening at an accelerating rate, you have no children at all, Darwin's demands feel like old and disturbing dreams, full of feeling yet strangely nonrelevant. From the perspective of middle age, the behavioral science of the first thirty-five years, the *first cycle* of human development, seems like an account of the dances of aborigines.

I received a large and early dose of the instinctual philosophy of the first cycle. A young child during the Watsonian era of behaviorism, a reading father who himself had no father after the age of four to teach him about the intuitive and messy operations of being a real father, a mother needing to produce successful children who loved her for it, I had a job to do. This orientation of all middle-class America was even more rigidly expressed in the families of immigrant Jews who were making a multigeneration effort at upward mobility.

The messages of Darwin and Freud were written in my loins. I practiced music four hours a day from fear. My father's words could wither. Before making love to a blond-haired, pink-nippled, soft, white-bellied lady, I had to own and jealously guard her. Images of World War II heroes, football stars, and interfraternity fights in high school combined with the excitement of her smell on my fingers to make reading about the primitive forces Darwin found on his voyage on the *Beagle* believable. Marxist economics, Machiavelli's directives, and the speeches of General Douglas MacArthur combined with a full feeling in the lower abdomen, a tight fist, grinding jaw, and a readiness to feel cornered and fight to make me a college freshman with Freud rather than Jung as my metaphysician. I thought I understood when the psychoanalyst Fenichel explained why some young men smelled girls' bicycle seats.

I saw man's paranoia as his most developed brain mechanism for survival. The capacity to anticipate danger, distant in time and space, became greater with the evolution of the primate forebrain, but it was there in primitive

COMING OF (MIDDLE) AGE / 9

form from the beginning. The rat, made more fearful with high doses of amphetamine, sniffs continuously in all directions for danger. The monkey on stimulants checks dark corners with ceaselessly oscillating eyes. The speed freak hides in the cellar from overhead bombers and buys a gun to protect himself from the newsboy member of the CIA. There is a paranoid baboon living in the middle of our brain.

Caring, need for attachment, group loyalty, and depressive pain at the loss of belonging keep the fiercely territorial and murderous human in a group. Hairless, slow, and weak, we couldn't have survived in any other way. Whereas the cocker spaniel left in a kennel can't eat or sleep from his pain of separation, Kipling's cat walks by himself and all places are the same to him. Unlike most dogs, the domesticated cat can hunt and survive alone.

Yet even in my time of first-cycle fire, strange things titillated my wonderings. I dismissed Jung's writings as anemic and delusional—yet a sentence or two would hit a high place in me, above the waist. Beethoven's Ninth done in a church left me with goose pimples but unshaken in the belief that religion was a perversion that occurred when normal genital discharge was blocked, the backup of sexual juices, frozen into icicles, making ecclesiastical illuminations in the brain. Eastern philosophies teaching detachment, compassion, and enlightenment I dismissed as carnival tricks of snake hypnosis, confused thinking from malnutrition of the brain, a reason for not doing anything in impossibly crowded countries.

Once in a while, during my medical training, a dying man would look back and seem to be saying something important, but I was too anxious to get close enough to ask. Jung, hypochondriacal from childhood, fainting with strong feelings, had death as a lifelong companion. He wrote that he never interviewed a patient over forty in whom mortality wasn't a dominant concern. I thought he was cowardly and forty was old. My mentor Freud, even when living in the smell of death from his rotting, cancerous jaw, never acknowledged its presence. He called the fear of death a disguise for a fear of injury to the penis or of not getting fed.

Darwin, Freud, and Marx were my men, the Vince Lombardi voices of our time. An erected phallus pointed the way to truth. It was the biology of survival. I did research on the brain, treated patients, and taught medical students, fortified by the songs of this virile chorus.

Then my life began to teach me about other things.

"I can't tell if he's crazy or if it's from the drugs. He shouted men's names all night." I saw the nursing supervisor of the coronary intensive care unit through the half glass wall of the nurses' station. The door was open and she was on the phone.

"He wanted to know the way into the second cycle. . . . No, I don't understand, either. He finally got to sleep on the extra morphine you ordered." She softened her voice. "Isn't it something? The chairman of our psychiatry department gets coronary pain and goes crazy. . . . The names? One of the night techs made a list. Henry Kissinger, Thelonious Monk, Armand Hammer, Alan Watts, Philip Roth, Sri Aurbindo, John Lilly, and some others she couldn't get. . . . OK. We'll be expecting you later." She hung up and sat hunched over my chart.

I was in one of the four beds on the unit. Yellow walls, sound-textured ceiling, and a cluster of electronic machinery surrounded our plastic-tented beds. On my night table were two plants and a bunch of flowers that startled me. I hadn't seen a country bouquet with bluebells for a long time. They were the same as those that were hidden, unidentified, among the dense, funereal collection that surrounded me ten years before when I woke up after my cancer surgery.

I didn't remember what happened last night or much about the men. There were brief periods of euphoric clarity mixed with muddled confusion, frightening images, and an occasional familiar face. The other patients were asleep. Bottles dripping, lighted monitors humming, we looked like dogs, helpless on our backs, in my medical school's physiology laboratory. I could hear the monotone of the professor: "In this condition, the blood pressure can go up, go down, or stay the same." The shrewd, old cardiovascular physiologist was at work disabusing us of the hope for a definitive knowledge of the heart. He had lived long enough to know that the heart will always know more about us than we shall know about it.

When I first felt the pain between my shoulder blades, it was little and mysterious, but enough to get me to a cardiologist, enough to motivate dieting and running, enough to reduce my smoking, enough to send me into the deepest depression of my life. From a labile life of surprises, I found myself in the endless waiting of wooden miles of sameness for a death that was inexorable. By the time it arrived it wouldn't need a sword, a broom would suffice for the dried-out and crumbled thing I was becoming.

One day the pain became something else. It squeezed my chest with bear arms. I tried to keep running and I couldn't. I ran a few more steps. Sudden and undeniable nausea and then vomiting on the beach. I dragged myself home and, fighting the knowledge, I lay down. It didn't help. I was soaked in sweat and reviewing my knowledge of cardiovascular reflexes. My heart was beating too fast. I shot an emergency syringe of Demerol into my thigh. The warm flush didn't touch the pain and my panic swamped the drug's euphoria.

I had played with the little chest pain for months. Every morning when I was running those miles. Too fast and a balloon would swell in my chest. I'd walk until it subsided. Every day I could run a little farther before my warning friend spoke. I ran longer each morning and put two syringes of Demerol in my medicine chest in case. When the second injection didn't help, I called an ambulance and passed out.

This morning I awoke on the barren plateau beyond Darwin's climactic hill of fighting and fucking—a land I first saw ten years ago when I waited to die of testicular cancer and which I forgot as soon as possible. Here it was again. Complete with a bouquet of bluebells.

TWO

When I hear an orchestra warming up, a large one, I think of the brain and its parts. The air fills with cascades of exercises, violins over difficult passages, trombones doing up-downs, a trumpet's scream for attention, a mumbling almost below hearing bowed on the bass viol. This polyglot of voices, separate and free running, soon would be harnessed to deliver the massive message of the evening's symphony. The polyphonic sounds of a human brain orchestra can also be fused in a creative moment and an act of intimacy or, directorless and without a score, its voices run free in the senseless chattering of a movie sound track of insanity.

Many of us working in neurobiology think of the human brain as composed of three sections, each part of the gathered history of our evolutionary development and arranged in concentric layers like an onion. The oldest and innermost of these brains is reptilian. It has machinery for the reflex control of muscles, glands, guts, heart, and blood vessels, as well as a permanently wired system that runs more complex instinctual activities like eating and mating.

The middle brain—I call it the dog brain—is common to all mammals, encircles the snake brain, and is in charge of a more flexible set of activities for individual and species survival such as hunting and fighting for food, emergency operations, sexuality, interpersonal connectedness, and group behavior such as tribal membership and dominance. We know these things from electrical stimulation of the brain in monkeys and man and the words of epileptics who fire off this lobe and tell us how it felt.

The outer layer of the onion, the upper brain, is the place used by high primates and man for intention, anticipation, thinking, problem solving, abstract learning, and verbal communication.

The distinctions made are ones of emphasis: reptiles learn and communicate; dogs anticipate danger. Some neurological theorists say that each of the three brains has all the capacities, but with more symbolic function and abstraction possible at each higher evolutionary stage.

Human behavior comes from these three brains in simultaneous motion, each with a karmic will of its own, running with various degrees of engagement with the others. Does some magic driver coordinate it all, or is that just a fantasy? Perhaps the word *coordination* is not justified. Perhaps the concept of the holographic integration of the brain is an optical illusion, the most flagrant example of the human denial of randomness since the invention of the phrase "I have decided." Maybe the report of the integrated function of the human brain is propaganda from the upper brain, which can always be counted on to make sense out of whatever we find ourselves doing.

My reptile brain feels so rigid that I can't talk to it with much influence—though there are some whose years of practice have allowed them to control their heartbeat and blood pressure. The modern instrumentation of "feedback" appears to help with this learning by talking back to this mute snake brain without words.

My upper brain, the place of higher intellectual activity, is a reference source of techniques useful in achieving the wishes of the middle brain. It's also a facile generator of excuses. It has never felt like the boss. The power of this upper brain puzzles me. It is the neural substrate of our culture (the place we'll carry our books when a ruler burns our libraries) with its advanced science, technology, art, and communicational skills. But, with all that capacity, it acts like the meek follower of the wishes of the middle brain. It certainly did during the first thirty-five years of my life. Maybe new capacity can be found in it. Is it possible that this cool, elaborate upper brain is the place of a wise, beautiful, and restful life, the location of the second cycle?

The middle brain's convolutions surround the lower brain. The relative constancy in size and shape of the middle brain throughout phylogeny contrasts with the rapid evolution of the upper brain, growing and twisting at a great rate with the successive emergence of species. Part of the middle brain is hungry and dedicated to the *self-preservative* functions of food seeking (smelling, mouthing, chewing, eating), sensing danger, and brooking no interference. Another group of functions are called *species-preservative* and run on sexual feelings. In monkeys these include grooming, pleasure reactions to genital stimulation, penile erections, sexual postures in females, courtship behavior, tribal and family arrangements for the safety of children, and fear and depression as responses to loss. In man, this brain part underlies everything from rearing and protecting the family to the building of hospitals for the altruistic pleasure of taking care of others. The middle brain's theme of *individual survival* blends well with Freud's concept of *id*. It's more difficult without several hours of Talmudic discussion to see that Freud's concept of *superego*, though garnished in expression by societal values and norms, finds its blindly instinctual roots in the neurological substrates of *species survival*. Sexual and territorial jealousy expressed in law and righteous rage are examples.

Much of my personal and professional life had been spent struggling with the first-cycle issues of the middle brain. From this perspective, the authority of the upper brain has sounded like so much braggadocio, the macho claims of a little, bespectacled professor. Freud's theories of instinct are the romance of the middle lobe. The major source of dynamic conflict, called id-versus-superego by Freud, called impulse-versus-delay of response by his followers, is buried in the complexities that social organization created by co-opting the middle brain's polarity between individual and species survival. Usually, when two such strong underlings have a difference of opinion they go to their boss. One might think that middle-brain conflict would be taken to the upper brain for resolution. Until very recently I didn't think that the upper brain could decide anything. When the cognitive theorists talked about upper-brain decision-making, I thought about the hot air of debate in the United Nations General Assembly during a Middle East crisis 'of war. Upper-brain output was the practice of an art form, intellectualization, that man uses to fill up time until instinctual clash or burnout occurs. Until very recently I saw life as a battle in the middle brain which species survival won. Fish swim upstream to lay eggs and die smashed on the rocks. Octopus mothers stop eating after their progeny emerge from their eggs. Human mothers become depressed when their children leave home—some use suicide to still the pain of the relentlessly rotating beacon searching for a lost child. Businessmen die of coronaries while making our system work. Ants cross a rivulet by the first several hundred drowning, their bodies forming a bridge. I feel helpless when seeing the twisted human expressions of the middle brain's bipolarity in my office: sadomasochism; erotic but puritanical judgmentalness; good boys torturing dogs; hungry anorexics; church-elder children's-park exhibitionists; pridefully housebound yet lonely isolates.

My most recent source of hope, the upper brain, detached from the middle-brain monster, feels weak but unconflicted: the mastery of a jigsaw puzzle, the aesthetic elegance of a well-done mathematical proof, the joy of symmetry and closure in thought and art, amusement at distant foibles, and best of all, the flying ecstasy of a creative leap. Freud first, and, most poetically, Erik Erikson, proposed an area of psychic function that sounds detached from the conflicts of the middle lobe. Not everyone agrees. Is a surgeon a middle-brain sadist? Or an altruistic saver of lives whose nipple-biting, anal-squeezing, first-cycle, middle-brain rage-energy has cooled and frozen into dependable surgical instruments? The creative leap for life from the first to the second cycle may be an escape from the cauldron of the middle brain to the playground of the upper brain.

"Time for a sponge bath, Arnie." Through the plastic wall of my tent and in the shadows created by a small night-light, I saw Carole, a professor of nursing with whom I'd taught in years past. Tall, blond, strong-featured, and with the firm and big fullness of the Scandinavians, her repartee was sexual and brusque. The students laughed at our dialogues. Doctor-nurse fantasies peopled their middle-brain circuits where the behind-as-medical-playground and parental no-nos are located. We hadn't been physically intimate for almost ten years. She had sent the wild flowers.

"I wondered if you would come. The first things I saw were the bluebells. Why so late? What time is it?"

"Two in the morning." She was making suds with a washcloth in a large metal bowl. Nursing faculty dress in street clothes and wear long white coats. Carole was wearing a nursing uniform.

"Hey, I'm not going to die. Did you make a special trip to anoint me for the grand passage? . . . Well, you're . . ." I stopped suddenly when I saw the caring in her face.

"I've been calling. They said that you didn't make any sense. Thrashing around. They had a tough time getting you to stay in bed." She spoke quietly and continued to make suds.

"My memory is so fragmented. Bits and pieces. I don't know whether it's the drugs or . . ."

"They say that you were yelling about escaping the

brain and asking some men to help. You accused Pete Rozelle of hiding your heart under a cup in a shell game."

Carole unzipped the tent, gently pulled off my pajama shirt, and began to soap my chest. I remembered the last time I had a craziness about a shell game. It was ten years before and a month before my thirty-first birthday when my left testicle, containing a lethal form of cancer, was removed. I was getting over the first procedure, waiting the two days until they were going to open my abdomen from navel to backbone to clean out everything that was loose, when I got paranoid about the hospital staff. Coming out of general anesthetic, disoriented by pain medication, terrified about the statistical tables that wouldn't stop appearing in my head, I hallucinated. I saw my kindly surgeon become a carnival psychopath playing a shell game with my testicle on the dinner tray. I actually saw him. His cruel smile, my frantic efforts to keep track of the quick movements. I screamed out in fright. After the second operation I had the machinery for erection but lost the nerves to ejaculate.

Her hands were so gentle. How could such a big-boned and feisty woman feel so tentative and soft? She watched my face. I was tipped on my side, and the warm wet cloth over my back felt good. The curtains were drawn around my bed and I enjoyed the respite from the electronic battlefield.

I remembered another shell game, my first. My father had given me permission to take my girlfriend to the fair. Saturday's music practicing, homework, and house chores over, I received final clearance to enjoy myself. In a fourteen-year-old's state of omnipotence, ready to exhibit my guile, I took on the man near the gate who was working the shell game. I winked at blond and pretty Lois as I invested my bankroll for big winnings. Less than five minutes later, humiliated beyond comforting, I took her home with the bus fare that remained. Are losing a testicle, ejaculation, a circulatory pump, and money in front of my lady the same thing? Some analysts would have it so.

A psychoanalytic invitation to escape from the fear of dying to the drama of losing a pissing contest brings relief. But it's not the truth. Heroic, cowardly Freud never addressed the distant but inexorable rumble of approaching death . . . only the masking whines of a loser.

The oscilloscopic screen peeked over Carole's shoulder as she turned me toward her. The traveling green dot was synchronized with the beat of my heart; its rate was displayed like the time of day by a digital clock. I reached beneath her skirt to feel the inside of her stockinged leg. She continued her washing. My hand moved up to cup her. It was a warm place. I moved my hand gently and soon felt her slick welcome. She rolled me on my back and pulled up the legs of my pajama bottoms. She washed my feet and legs. My muscles began to give up their tense readiness; I felt a warmth creeping into my abdomen from below, a dreamy float out of this hospice of death to a life that had been forgotten. Her breathing got faster. Then, suddenly, the fullness in my back arrived, with a thin, sharp jab on top. The green dot was racing; the clock read 143. She looked at the oscilloscope and nodded her head in acknowledgment but not in alarm. The pain slipped away. She helped me back into my pajama top and zipped the tent. She sat watching me as I rested. I was asleep when she left.

The night nurse was in later with my syringe of Dilaudid. I was staring at the ceiling. My two sons were almost independent, but maybe humans didn't have to swim upstream and smash themselves on the rocks; maybe there's something left after laying our eggs. But once out of the first cycle's brain, was there anywhere else? The smell of her on my fingers registered in my middle brain, my old home. Male dogs, chasing such scents, kill each other to claim its source. Is there another way?

The Dilaudid made things soft. Braced against the hard edge of another assault of pain and driven by my restless head machine, I welcomed the cushion. The ceaseless meter of the little green dot had been the cadence of my life. A clock, a timetable, a metronome.

"We have to get this part perfect." My mother's smile was excited. "This Sunday you play a concert for your father. It's the end of summer, and he must hear what you've accomplished." The metronome was a rhythmic claim.

Fidgety boredom became the nausea of fear. Sunday's music critic, black-mustached, had fierce brown eyes and a whim of iron. My mother, master piano professor, presented his Stalinesque charisma as an incipient danger. Only a perfect pianistic rendition would earn safety from swamping diatribes.

At first, the opiate smoothed the restless march of sharp and endless thoughts, giving me a place to stand in quiet rationality. Then, from below the belly button, the lazy haze became a rushing, rising highway of euphoria, faster and faster. I would make it! Out of this place of death. Optimism, at first tentative, became a moving train of power. I was wise and infinite, strolling thoughtfully in a pair of loosely strung white cotton pants, a flowing cotton madras shirt, and sandals. A new savant. Beyond the valley of agitated despair, I climbed the path to a beautiful view. In chemical peace I saw beyond the middle brain to a new time, a new place, a new brain. Dilaudid gave me a peek at a future.

How did Mary stand it? Four in the afternoon on Saturday, after a full week of twelve-hour days in medical school and enough anxiety about it to eliminate closeness, and what was I doing? Renewing our intimacy with steamed crabs and talk at Lake Pontchartrain? Taking her to Farmers' Market for light chicory and doughnuts? No. I was in a neurophysiology laboratory with my cats, working on the neural mechanism of consciousness. The electrodes were planted in the brain in places that could move the cat from a purring sleep to a hair-standing alertness for danger. The sweeping green dot of the oscilloscope, as always, was my drummer. The electroencephalograph's writing in red ink tracked on unrolling paper was the permanent record of music the cat and I were making. Becoming a doctor was not enough to still my frightened itch of ambition. I needed to find God and He was reported to be in the brain.

Weekend afternoons in a small dark room in the basement of the basic sciences building. One dim bulb and a row of dirty basement windows cast dingy light on a calico cat with long wires running from his brain to a mountain of electronic machinery. Consciousness had gotten complicated. Weeks before, I noticed that when the current to awake the sleeping cat was increased, the animal squirmed and then cried out in discomfort. After the switch was turned off, he looked at me questioningly, as though he wanted something. At first I didn't get the message. Then one day I realized that the cat always returned to the place on the floor where he was standing when he last got the stimulation. Was he seeking the arousing, painful stimulation? Olds and Milner from Montreal had already reported that animals would learn to bar-press to receive electrical stimulation of their brains, but they talked about pleasure. I didn't know they'd do it for pain. Was I getting close to my fascination with my father? The teeth in the clock? The middle-brain man in the metronome?

Fatigue, compulsion, aloneness, and the aroma of cat shit and ammonia. Paper with red squiggles piling up on the floor. Green dot sweeping. I searched this dungeon for my salvation, mind racing to explain with brain-wiring diagrams, feedback loops, switches whose thresholds change with use, gland juices containing world views. With a stiff back and fatigued fingers, I was playing on the piano of the brain, looking for an escape from the restless pain that the cat told me was attractive. My psychoanalyst would later call me an adrenalin addict: a depressive looking for an upper who would settle for fright.

My childhood friends asked me, "Do you like your

father?" Tyrannized and fear-roped to a rack of endless output, I couldn't come out to play. No sports, casual talk, afternoons at Monopoly, or masturbating in a circle with my buddies unless it could be explained as constructive. My friends wanted me to say that he was a son of a bitch. The vomit-ready excitement and fear triggered by the smell of his cigar as he drove up the driveway should have driven me out at a much earlier age. The explosive temper, the flashing eyes, the cross-examinations, the lectures into the night, the fear. I said that I laid low until I had the strength to get out. That I paid pain for safety might be closer to the truth. It's written that way in the middle brain.

The American Physiological Association's fall meetings were in Rochester, New York, and I was twenty-two and making my first pilgrimage to see the wise men. Mary and I would stop to see my relatives in Washington, D.C., visit the neurophysiology laboratories of the National Institute of Mental Health, camp through the Shenandoah and the Finger Lakes region, and I would give the first scientific paper of my career. She asked me if during this trip, our first vacation, we could share some respite from my efforts to dig a tunnel through the brain. Could we talk of other things? Anything. Even *her* patience had been worn thin. What had happened to her flying intellectual companion of the Stanford days? She couldn't root me out. She tried astrophysics, pornography, and politics. She played Monk and Miles and tried to reliven my old theory about the latent racial anger in Charlie Parker's flatted fifth chord. Head boxed into obsession, I answered with talk about the neural location of the homunculus of pitch. A walk through Audubon Park on spring evenings of orange blossoms and honeysuckle brought out-loud ruminations about the decreasing role of smell in the conduct of man's social affairs, about what had moved into the middle brain when smelling activity left, when seeing and hearing rather than aroma took over as the trigger for love and paranoia. She led me to the zoo in the park, and we stood in front of the male baboon, busy cowering his two females. An articulate libber since the early 1950s, she stood in front of the cage and made faces. She swore at him and called him my father. Wealthy, he had rejected my marriage by withdrawing financial support. Marriage, like masturbation, drained the strength of young men and made them crazy. I drew the neurophysiological pathways of aggression on the sidewalk in front of the cage, and she walked away in despair.

We were up early in the autumn crispness. The trees in the New York mountains, leaves turned burnt orange and yellow, were frosted. We slept on the ground in a deserted campground overlooking Lake Seneca. I remember the stillness. Stiff from a night in sleeping bags, we took a walk to warm up. A path led through the trees to an edge. Suddenly there was a long and narrow, deep, dark blue lake far below, ringed with evergreens and pines, the fluffy clouds in diffuse pink from the rising sun, and it was quiet. I saw it. My ceaseless head rattle stopped and I took a peek out of my middle brain. For a few moments I lifted my eyes from the sewing machine of my grandfather doing piecework, the demands of my father, my electrical brain factory, my jerry-built brain theories, my sore-brained narcissism. The sight brought tears, and I wanted to run. It gave me, congenitally blind, a few moments of kaleidoscopic sight, a flashing review of all the prettiness I'd never seen: I explained it away as quickly as possible in information-processing terms. The visual imprint of mountain lake, coming during an accidental moment of silence of the survival brain, brought tears as an incidental brain-stem correlate of the emotional charge necessary to establish memory. It was the computer command PRINT and nothing else.

We were in the cheap student clothes of the mid 1950s. My uncle was in a gray sharkskin suit, blue suede shoes, silk shirt, the biggest white Cadillac in Washington, D.C., and charming nouveau riche manners. We were being driven to the National Institutes of Health by a man who started with a small grocery store in the 1930s and now led one of the largest meat-purveying chains in the country. His dark mustache and flashing eyes evidenced his membership in that labile and temperamental strain to which my father belonged. Fear seems to run in families and is often called dominance. He was taking his nephew, the medical student, and his graduate student wife to see a government research institute. Proudly.

Mary and I tried to explain what research was about. Sitting at a country-club dinner, we spoke of John Lilly's work in the brain. My uncle asked about the purpose of research. We had some trouble at first, given his high tax bracket, but eventually we found that his company prized its most creative butcher who invented new sausages. "New product development" sounded good to him, until he asked what we were selling. I had a similar problem with my grandmother, years later. She asked me why her psychiatrist grandson was so poor. I explained about being a professor and doing research. She nodded, but without much conviction. Later I overheard her explaining my circumstances in a phone conversation with a friend. "I'm not exactly sure what biochemical research is, but I think it's a thing that from fifty thousand dollars you make dreck."

John Lilly was tall, slim, gray suited, and busy. It was several years before his days as a guru for Simon and Schuster. He had many experiments going simultaneously. One was the self-stimulation paradigm. He was trying it in monkeys. He took Mary, Uncle Al, and me to the laboratory. A wall of electronic equipment was on one side of a darkened and quiet room. A monkey was sitting in a restrictive chair. In the darkness, red lights, green-lighted scope faces, and staring research assistants gave me the impression that something invisible was happening. Lilly explained that the monkey was being trained to press a bar for stimulation in the middle brain. At first the monkey seemed relaxed. Then he became more active, looking from side to side. He suddenly pressed a lever near his right hand. He looked startled as though struck, and then screamed in pain. Over and over as though it weren't ever going to stop. And then, as when a child has cried for a long time, the screams became breathless whimpers and disappeared. Mary sat transfixed. The humanness of monkeys compared to cats made it startlingly painful. Lilly was calmly watching the emerging record on paper. Uncle Al looked frightened. The monkey remained quiet for several moments. Then the restlessness began again. He began his visual checking of the corners and finally pressed the bar—another burst of screams. Mary mumbled under her breath about the importance of the discovery. Lilly began to talk about Brady's work at Walter Reed Hospital which had shown very much the same thing. I had begun to speculate about the neurophysiology of masochism. Uncle Al was pacing back and forth behind us with his hands in his pockets. I had never seen him so upset.

"What the hell's wrong with you guys? Are you showing that a monkey likes to be hurt? If you bullshitters don't know by now that people do stuff they don't want to, then you should go back to grammar school. You guys! You guys!" He walked toward the door and opened it as he was speaking. "You guys got something wrong with you. The monkey's OK. I'm getting the hell out of here, and don't tell anybody I've been here. I'll be downstairs." He slammed the door.

I was embarrassed and watched the floor. There was a long silence. Lilly finally spoke. "You know, I think your Uncle Al might be right. Maybe what we do is find out what we know already. What do we need all this equipment for?" I thought he was kidding. When years later he got rid of his oscilloscopes and dolphins, I realized he wasn't.

From the stale bread and honey on cold mornings after nights on the ground to the luxury of my uncle Al's country club. Our car had been stocked by my aunt for the second phase of our camping trip. She didn't understand, or did she? Canned mushrooms, herring from the Bering Strait, kosher salami, German chocolate bars, and enough triple-decker sandwiches to last for a week. They offered to pay for rooms with hot baths the rest of the way; they couldn't understand why we slept on the ground. Pride and a feeling of mission wouldn't allow us to accept. Not so many years later, this incident forgotten, I railed at the hypocrisy of hippies in forty-dollar, preworn jeans.

A nurse was standing in front of me with a little white cup and some water.

"Dr. Mandell. We've switched your medicine to oral and I'm late. I didn't want to awaken you." She unzipped my tent and I took the tablet.

"I think I have a disease caused by the wars of the middle brain. But maybe not all power is bad. Kissinger power kills. Maybe Castenada power can save." The nurse was shaking her head as though she didn't understand. I was still foggy from the opiate. It sounded sensible enough to me.

"I'm not too sure what you're saying, but you're supposed to stay as quiet as possible. They're going to send a psychiatrist to talk to you very soon."

"A psychiatrist? It won't help. Ten years ago when I had my testicle removed, my analyst came to see me. Do you know what he did? He offered me a job. I think psychiatrists are more afraid of death than their patients are. Who are they going to send?"

"Kapilloff. Dr. Ronald Kapilloff."

"Well, it could be a lot worse." Kapilloff was probably

the best psychotherapist in the department. What could I tell him? That I couldn't fight anymore? That if I didn't find some other place to live, I would have to kill myself? Maybe I would just ask him why *he* gets up in the morning. I could hear him now. He'd say the question wasn't a question but a symptom.

THREE

After thirty-five, a penis becomes more difficult to train and impossible to command. Like a car's motorized antennae it requires a live battery, the ignition key turned, and someone to push the right button. If all the things aren't working, it won't function. You can pull on it all you want.

Voluntary brain systems—pick up the hammer and hit the nail—feel as though they're controlled by decision. In the case of a doctor's son with a high IQ who dropped out of medical school to become a carpenter, how much was deciding and what was unconscious resentment is a question for the philosophers. Involuntary brain systems—stomach squeezing, heart speeding—feel as though they're out of our control, though staying in a job that causes both seems like a matter of choice. When we get to a neuromuscular apparatus that involves both voluntary and involuntary elements—turn on the faucet *and* relax the sphincter to start a nervously hesitant urinary stream—we find an arena of enormous potential for the symptoms of the ambivalent. In the case of the penis, we have an involuntary system of erection and ejaculation, the voluntary moving of hips and squeezing of the sphincters, *plus* an intrinsic confusion in the regulatory chemistry making some kinds of excitement helpful for performance and others paralytic. The penis brain can't fake it. It will only work as a willing partner, though sometimes its carrier has to learn that it's willing. To talk about what to do with an uncooperative penis is like planning to have a good time. Whatever good sense the thoughts may make, you'll have to wait and see.

Most of the difficulty with the penis, when there is difficulty, is with its connections. The penis brain doesn't exist in isolation. *Playboy*'s attempt to make it so by objectification—a good beer, a fine watch, a pair of tits—makes for great looking but is hopelessly dumb about function. The penis is in the middle brain and hooked up to a lot of doing besides fucking. If the other things aren't working, the penis won't either.

In the squirrel monkey, the things that lead to penile erection and display (sticking it in the other monkey's face in a head-to-tail, stereotyped posture) include: meeting a strange animal (sizing each other up), seeing themselves in a mirror, courting, and establishing dominance over other male members of the tribe (driving around in a big car). The part of the brain that represents penile erection and display is intimately tied to the species-survival functions of the middle brain. These include courting, mating, and making and maintaining family and tribal arrangements. Activation of these neurons not only produces erection, pieces of these social behaviors, but pleasure. Animals and men will stimulate themselves endlessly through electrodes placed in these sites. Men describe abdominal warmth, euphoric states, and a full, satisfied feeling. The middle brain is arranged so that we get rewarded with sexual pleasure for exercising our social responsibilities. Or, to put it another way, deep in the brain, sexual pleasure is linked to a sense of responsibility: a feeling of obligation to protect mate, children, and territory, to be close and to go to war. Many men and women with penis troubles are people who don't want to buy into all of that.

Much of the psychiatry of the past half-century has come from the penis and has therefore promised an expertise in the area. To the extent that neurotic anxiety is the trouble, the practitioners can often help. Worry about impotence is the commonest cause of impotence—so that turning the patient's attention away from the "superficial and obviously-going-to-get-well symptom" of impotence to a "real" problem with his mother may cure him by distraction.

When the psychotherapist doesn't respect the fundamentals of the penis brain, however, he's ineffective. Social theorists have suggested open marriage as a solution to the current crisis in social-sexual roles. Open marriage leads to emotional divorce because to violate the brain system that requires territoriality for penile erections is to lead eventually to no erections, after the novel excitement from jealous rage and homosexual sandwiches is used up. The grown-up middle brain is tough. What can psychotherapists' talk do for the middle brain of a bank president who chose humiliation, ruination, and suicide over ceasing his practice of shocking little girls with his penile display? Six doctors seemed not to know. The forty-seven-pound, fifteen-year-old girl was hyperactive, argumentative, rational, stubborn, quick-witted, adroitly manipulative, and wouldn't eat. When she did, she vomited and took a high colonic. When asked what she was doing, she said she was making herself beautiful. In the days when talk was the treatment for anorexia nervosa, the death rate approached fifty percent. Drug treatment of these twisted monuments to the power of the middle brain has significantly reduced fatalities.

Penis behavior in men and women is a piece of naked brain sticking out for all to see. Undefended. It's taught me a deep respect for neurobiology and about the powerlessness of much of our talk.

The brain, like the sun and other stars, has its own system of organization. We should stop pretending that we can control it. The first psychiatrists, like the first astrological priests, were suitably overwhelmed by the power of their subject: the stars and brain as God. They moved tentatively. The generations of practitioners who followed couldn't live with the ambiguity. The demands of the customers and the glittery rewards of their role were too great. They made up logical systems of thought that implied that the astral gods and the brain were understood. They sold their services as spokesmen. In the cosmologies they created, all was understood. Humbling, direct contact with the enormity of the phenomena and the knowledge of our fundamental helplessness were lost. But delusion can last only as long as the life of the first madman and the political strength of his institutions. Our needs have gotten more desperate, the half-lives of the madmen's theories grow shorter, the solutions more bizarre. I heard on the radio one day about a "growth" seminar that was to be held which would feature guided group discussion, hypnosis, Synanon games, est, dream analysis, Gestalt, massage, exercise, and meditation. All for one hundred and fifty dollars. Viewing the now quickly shifting fads of schools of psychotherapy within a collapsed time frame, the kind that makes the Jurassic period seeable on the wall of one's room, reveals that each new plan to control the brain god with talk is an unseeable speck that comes and goes with the rapidity and lack of residue of a hairstyle.

It's time that we soul doctors acknowledged our know-nothing confusion again.

"Hey, Arn!" Ron Kapilloff is a bear of a man at six feet one and two hundred twenty pounds. Thoughtful and exquisitely sensitive, he hides under a superficial manner of bumbling earnestness. Those with faster thyroids find themselves taking over what he's trying to say. Of course that works very well with patients, since people believe their own words. Director of the department's education program, his kindness led to a nickname of Big Tits. No one knew that when playing New York City basketball he was often ejected for rough play. We interviewed patients together in Grand Rounds easily and without preparation. There was comprehension and respect between us, a never-stated closeness. Standing by my bed, he looked uncomfortable.

"They sent you because you wouldn't rattle the beast."

"Come on, Arn. I came up to visit."

"Bullshit! Weren't you talking to the head nurse on the phone?" He nodded. "You and I don't have to play games. A shrink gets chest pain and goes out of his head."

He pulled the drape around my bed and sat down. "OK, Arn. What's going on?"

"I've got to get out. Away from my brain. The one that's held me prisoner. The paranoid thing that won't let me leave my guard post long enough to feel. I have to get from the olfactory brain to the part of the frontal neocortex that . . ."

"Geez, Arn, before you get into one of your theories, don't you think you ought to let me know what's happening? I haven't seen you in months. The people in your laboratory say you've been depressed."

"Depressed? What it feels like is that I no longer exist. My head whirls around my sons, my relationships with women, my ex-wife, the department, my career, psychiatry, research, the smearing of my name in the war with the NFL about its drug policies, a whole bunch of stuff. But it's more than all that—and less." Ron nodded. Waiting.

"How about a diagnosis of coronary artery disease at the age of thirty-nine? Getting put on some medicine that almost killed what was left of my sex life after the cancer surgery. King Kong feelings about my potency have turned into scary games of roulette with my dick. But I don't always feel so down. Sometimes I see it all as a path to a new high place. Freedom. Beauty. But the feeling doesn't last very long. I'll tell you what to put down on the chart: 'Life stresses have exacerbated the manifestations of a basically cyclothymic personality leading to a prolonged period of depression and then the beginnings of a manic

break at the time of a threatened heart attack.' Just put
that down and they'll leave you alone. They'll come in
here wanting to put me on lithium, and then I'll kill myself. That's all you have to . . ."

"Wait. Not so fast. I'm here to take off some of the
heat. They're scared to death. To have a psychiatrist go
crazy in his own hospital is like a lion tamer turning his
animals on the audience. Let's stop talking like psychiatrists. What's really been happening, Arn?" He sat un-
ruffled, chin resting on his hand. It's a good combination
in a psychiatrist: basketball toughness and gentle per-
sistence. Where should I begin?

My time had been spent running frantically through
dark and ambiguous places, shadowed by a low-lying cloud
of fear. Pridefully unwilling to seize any metaphysical solution, I also lacked the courage to live as though I had. The
toughness of brain science affords grounds for cynical,
daylight laughter, but is a comfortless companion for
middle-of-the-night panic and early morning dread. I was
looking for a message. Could I hear it above the nervous
noise of my head?

It began a while back. My brain hormones, life-set in
an oscillating rhythm of hibernation after generative times
of plenty, hit a new low. There was no energy. My older
son had taken violent leave of the family fire circle to
take his own turf. A tenuously supported, mutually held
delusional system that backed my marriage's contract for
coupling first grew depleted with long and desperate use
and then disappeared. The cosmic feeling of specialness
that came from doing scientific research and rescuing patients became the boredom of everyday work. There wasn't
any saving greatness.

As forty approached, I could run no longer, My tense
life got unstrung, in a succession of snaps, wire strings
tangling up in coils of confusion. I was left with unanswer-
able questions in place of knowledge, no inspirational
direction, and a desire to silence the instrument forever.
There were endless ruminations about how and why it

all started, how I got here, and what it was all about. The usual bounce out of bed and the arrogant knowing that if I couldn't outthink, I could outrun, were all gone. All the running I could do was with my legs. My head wouldn't move; rather, it sat in front of the mess with the stubborn air of ultimatum. My brain wouldn't let me hide my questions in a quickly built set of psychiatric explanations, behind a neon storefront of denial. I might be able to sell it to my customers, but I couldn't buy. My head waited for a *real* reason. In this clouded, restless, and empty state, I worked in my laboratories, a shaman looking for a self-cure, searching for soul-active substances in a foliage of glassware. After so many years of work, surely the brain would tell me something. I needed it now. Then a heart pain let me know that my time was disappearing. My need to do rather than be done to took me into a car late one night in which only a last-minute, cowardly turn kept me from going over a cliff.

"I don't know where to begin, Ron. Last night I was flooded with the energy of sudden freedom. Like going through a barrier of fear into a land of choice. But the barrier is up again."

"Is it about dying?"

"The cancer time was terrifying. This is different. It's flat, empty. The fullness of my fantasies has become nothing. I'm anchored, but to what? If I can just get unstuck. The divorce felt the same. The family feeling of belonging, the things-are-as-they-should-be contentment of the middle brain, was harder to leave than Mary. For us, I knew it was time. For the blind clan loyalty of my ape brain, it could never be time. I want to take a real look at death and then move into a new life. I can't get my ass in gear. There's a blackness over my shoulder that I'll have to face, and I don't have the strength."

"Arn, I think this is important stuff." He wasn't here to cool the ward staff; he was here to treat a madman. What seemed at night like a moment of clarity, a peek at a fresh page, they saw as insanity. I've always been suspicious of ecstasy. The brief glimpses I've had of it felt so free and unobligated, not socialized. It can get out of control. A few sensitive women in my life knew that I couldn't stop monitoring and manipulating their crescendo to orgasm. "Don't you ever let go?" When I finally did, they thought I was crazy.

I remember my first depression and my first therapist. I was nine years old when I found Mrs. Flurkey. She was a wizened and chirpy high-school biology teacher in her late sixties. She lived next door and came out to meet me when I climbed over her fence to retrieve a ball. A lifelong Republican, she didn't understand my worshipful feelings about our President, FDR. We spoke of him at length when I snuck over to see her when things got too angry at my house. She panfried new potatoes in butter and parsley and served them with a cool glass of buttermilk and a genuine respect for my opinions. She told me that my beloved President was getting senile and explained what that meant in the brain. She told me that his brain disease had made him a dupe of the Communists.

I had been led by my father's cynicism to the belief that gods and their religions were the vehicles of the men behind them who wanted power. All my fears could be taken care of directly without the intermediary. My father or Roosevelt would take care of everything. The calm in FDR's voice during fireside chats kept the hordes of suicidal yellow men diving in airplanes and Aryan kick-step marching boots several stories high from coming into my bedroom window.

Then one day he died. I couldn't believe the news. No one I knew had ever died, and I didn't know that powerful people were subject to acts of nature. The sudden completeness of that feeling of *no more* filled me with an emptiness that I hadn't known before. How do you fix it? What do you do?

Disconsolate, I was without sleep or appetite. I rose

in the night to write poems about FDR. Mrs. Flurkey listened and then spoke about the biology of life cycles, the adaptive significance of death when a member of the larger social organism began to poison himself and others through the products of his aging physiology. Once your children had children, you served no purpose but energy consumption and environmental contamination. She said old people should live quietly and not take up too much of the sun. Once you were over forty, Charles Darwin didn't care about you anymore.

My mother took me to a pediatrician who said that I needed vitamins and to get away from my music practice for a while. My father delivered harangues about the need to keep going, no matter what. I wandered the neighborhood and couldn't play marbles, hide-and-seek, or even football. I claimed a lost dog named Scrappy, and he and I had long talks about Roosevelt. I fed him and felt better. Splinted by my relationship to Scrappy and Mrs. Flurkey's kindness, the hurt place gradually healed. But, like once surgically separated tissue, it always feels funny when I touch it.

"Ron, it's a question that won't leave me alone."

What of the intimacy of expert pair skaters? They respond to each other with such sensitivity and knowledge, but do they really know each other? Have they agreed to a complementary arrangement in which each relates to the other as fantasy? Is what looks to be real intimacy and understanding (no awkward missteps into each other's path, graceful comings together after complex goings away) just the expert conduct of a dance? Maybe mutuality is only in the eyes of the observer.

The stuck-together but intimately alienated pair creates a universe of relating that exists apart from either one. They live in the vision that others have of them. Was it always that way? Did it become that way? Did I make it that way?

The psychiatric articles on the incapacity of some

people with mood cycles to be other than distant from
their dear ones may apply. Depressed, they're afraid to be
close to the one they think is causing their pain. High,
they don't need anyone intimately. My ventures into
closeness feel like the insertion of a sharp hook under the
breastbone, pulled to pain at will by those whom I love
and who love me. My distance is an attempt at protection.
Is that the story with everyone? Joined, are we stranded
in robot fugues that seem to be us with others? Will there
always be a quiet, lonely, unsubstantial self, a nervous
ambiguity, the incipient presence of nothing? Or did I
kill a once-there thing? I believed in it wholly and would
have given my life for it not so long ago.

The dismantling of a long-lasting relationship brings
a different kind of disorientation than the loss of the
boundaries of an individual. The loss of the fixity of things
in one person is called schizophrenic confusion.

"The car was here. I worked all night. Where is it?
Who are those people patrolling the streets? Are they
looking for me? My car? I parked it yesterday morning.
Where is it? I'm going crazy." The panic rises and so does
the perplexity. A busy nervous buzz in the head, confusion, exists where calm thought used to be. "I walk
quickly, pretending. It will never stop. I see too deeply
into everyone, they look frightened and in pain. What did
I do? I'm going to need my car to escape." When the self
goes through a temporary collapse, the schizophrenia can
be slept off along with the sleep loss.

The collapse of a dyad feels like a loss of God, religion, meaning, social matrix, belief, sense of purpose.
The well-rehearsed rationales for living are dissolved in
the barely contained panic of anomie. The burning of
the flag of a life couple means, suddenly, that your beloved leader lies and steals. Your mother's only reason for
wanting you to succeed was so that you could support her.
God is run by hustling, homosexual Jesuit priests who
steal from poor Puerto Ricans to support their indulgent
dietary habits. The liquor industry buys legislators to pre-

vent programs for adequate prevention and treatment because their statistics have shown them that the twenty
percent who are alcoholic drink eighty percent of the
booze. The Federal Reserve System is a game of political
monopoly, and so is the Supreme Court. There is no truth,
beauty, or caring. Piano lessons and believing in Arrow-
smith as a child were silly. Humans are killers and eaters.
They talk to hide it.

"Ron, I need to know. Did I make it up? Was it ever
there?"

"I first found her . . . she found me . . . we found each
other . . . I was playing Ravel's *Boléro* on the big Baldwin
in the lobby of Branner Hall, the women's dorm."

Shy, fat, and ugly, I dressed to match. Baggy blue
balboas, dirty white shirt, muddy half-boots, and a blackened, once-brown suede jacket. The Stanford of that time
was short-haired, clean, Republican, beer, fraternity, and
football. My hair, curly, matted, fell to my shoulders. I
loved the sounds of Charlie Parker, Jack Kerouac, Lennie
Tristano, Ferlinghetti, Sri Aurobindo, and Alan Watts.
In 1951 that array filled the wide gap between me and the
fraternities. Even Jewish-dominated eating clubs, full of
soon-to-be lawyers, wouldn't lay claim to this early Stanford freak. I played bebop in all-night jam sessions at San
Francisco's Bop City with Barre Phillips and Pony Point-
dexter. Piano crazy, reefer blowing, eating fried chicken
and black ladies, I would barely get back to Stanford in
time for the next day's classes. As brave as all this sounds
for a seventeen-year-old freshman, it was cowardly. The
may-I games with Stanford women scared me far more.
Especially when they were pretty.

One day, I went to a women's dormitory and let my
jazz improvisation speak for me. My "Fine and Dandy"
was an Oscar Peterson dash across a little clearing; was
any female hunter interested? Kodály chords played in
somber time was my "Willow Weep for Me"; I'll be slow
and gentle. "My Funny Valentine," played in slim line
and easy baritone counterpoint, was taken from Mulligan

and Baker; lightness, I promise lightness; and all that my body could do. Kenton's "Artistry in Rhythm" gave me my moments of mounting, crashing chords and orgasmic release. Would someone listen to my piano? They sat around. Then she came.

She was delicate tissue, dainty pink petals. Pale, freckles, beautiful, brown eyes soft, brunette hair short, magical Audrey Hepburn on a rainy New York night, reading Nietzsche into the early hours, firmly upward breasts and intense. Eyes into mine and beyond, strange excitement, two smiles of recognition. What is it that we knew about each other? Late Beethoven string quartets, Prokofiev concertos, the role of Keynesian economics, the release of Zen. Even her Republicanism and commitment to the veracity of Whittaker Chambers (I was on the side of Alger Hiss) served only to demonstrate her loyalty to Palm Springs parents and served as a playground for teasing.

We did all that time's silly stuff. Argued about McCarthy, ate chocolate mint chip ice-cream cones, and believed in our personal success. She was strong and honest, discerning yet loyal, with the kind of Anglo-Saxon fire that, unlike the brief and searing flashes of the para-Mediterraneans, burns on forever. This was the time of football heroes, Bob Mathias, forever-after movies starring men on white horses, and the last proud march of the white male conquerors in America, the ones who brought rape and lifelong security to whomever we bedded.

It was amazing! The beautiful and brilliant young lady, who could have had anyone, chose me. She stared at me endlessly like a strange toy. I played the piano, watching her watch out of the corner of my eye. What could she be seeing that was making her happy? With one rivet, those eyes had recreated me. Bent funny by a funny family, feeling funny in my bentness, I stood up straight under her gaze. The no-me of childhood puppet performances, the no-man feeling of existence as achievement rather than person, disappeared in my appearance in her eyes. Her delight at my delighting kindled my capacity to delight and be delighted.

You mean my mother wasn't the only one? This time I was three thousand miles away from the mustached Giant of the Beanstalk and his frightened wife's assigned dances of obeisance. Free and known! Babied in my depressions, understood in my crazy searches, arousing her with my spread-eagled chords, I was proud, protective, and eager to earn it. Imagine, being in love without the requirement of school figures and ratings—1 to 10—by six judges. I began to grow to be worthy. Gone was the self-abnegation and delivery of what was asked at the price of who I was. For a while I even gave up my childhood pattern of agreeable dumbness that I had learned to use as a sign of my gratefulness for care. I was recreated in her vision without the price of becoming someone else. Hunger encompassed every available organ, spinal cord, thigh muscle, stomach, chest, shoulders, and then an explosion. And another. And another. In the wars that always bring peace.

"Or did I make all that up?"

"Is that state possible in this world?"

"Was it there once and now gone, or did I make it all up?"

We spent all our time together alone. Walking and talking, eating and sharing. Kandinski, Nijinsky, Ouspensky, Brubeck, Bach, and Bartók. So much of the interpersonal play of the I-felt-that-you-felt-that-I-felt-that-you-felt . . . the sex of psychoanalytic conversation . . . the pseudofights about Hull, Spence, and Skinner. She didn't believe that the brain is the cosmic jelly god of all that there is. I knew that it was.

I couldn't stand to be kept waiting. I paced, jealous and insecure, when she was late. Proud in the ownership of me, she trotted my head in conversational circles for her friends to see. A brilliant monster. Hunchbacked of brain, short of stature, intense of fucking, the dirty Jewish hippie with burning blue eyes who smelled so different from her two tennis-playing brothers. I was on the left. The left bank, the left hand of masturbation, the hairy Judas on the left of Christ. The starving and worthwhile cripple whom one can mother and feed by a joyful fucking that is altruistic. Do-gooding felt good, and she enjoyed the delicious, erotic forbiddenness of a Jewish Democrat— the same kind of electricity that would seduce the bred-out daughters of old wealth into the twisted hands of Manson and the SLA.

The princess had chosen me. It was a special act of God and I was grateful. Then, standing straight up for years, held by invisible strings to the balloons of our mutual fairy tale—the rehabilitated hunchback and the princess—I began to suspect that I had been sold out by my gratefulness. The price we charge is stamped on our foreheads early, and moving along into the next place, we teach that price to the new people, wondering how they found out. The ugly, bent freak object of my father's rages had strong feelings that were twisted up against the self so that anger out to make space inevitably brought along a recurrent path a feeling of worthlessness. The inevitable rubs of living together lit up that circuit. Rage. Then I'm awful. God damn it! Then forgive me. Move over. Then I'm piggish. Princess—crap! Then I'll kiss your foot. The jiggle back and forth, anger out, depression in, the biological reflex of anticipated retribution, moral machinations for ruminators like me, got bigger, oscillating in greater amplitude and for longer duration.

The princess had chosen me. It was a special act of God and I was grateful. But inside, a young voice, the early voice of my now voice, began to ask, wasn't I giving too? The missionaries gave penicillin to the natives after they said their prayers of thanks to the right God or they could just go die of pneumonia. Things were more complicated than I thought, or was it that they were simple? Had I brought my old ways with me? Head bowed in supplication after a burst of rage. Rational approaches brought the same lockstep argumentation that my father—had I married my father?—used to move me to pseudoinsightful surrender. Could I have created this waltz with a manikin?

The princess had chosen me. It was a special act of God and I was grateful. Excited and grateful. Owing. Was this the time that the young voice of self, forced out of my brain by my passions, took up residence in my spastic right colon? How could I resent a miracle? Several diagnostic rays couldn't find the angry voice, squeezing, resentful, in my right lower abdomen. It took twenty-two years, no, actually twenty-four years from the very beginning, for that voice to be heard.

"Ron, you're not answering. Did I make it up? The love? The specialness? The awfulness?"

Peaks of passion, sucking each other up with the primitive compulsion that leads to the inhaling of books, ice cream at night, and dope. There wasn't space to think. We were glued. She had become a piece of my brain. The truth and deception were two-layered: a middle-brain connection for life, an upper brain's talk of decision. We looked good at it for years and years.

Like expert pair skaters.

Digging furrows in the ground. Rooting. Planting. It was male business and had to be done. Hot and sweaty. Nervous. The pain of my erections radiates from the tip in a lightning trip through my left testicle (gone, but with a phantom presence) to the small of my back. It drives me away.

The pain started with my first erection after surgery. The chief resident in urology bet me a dollar that I wouldn't have an erection again. His eyes were tired. Was he challenging me in that shoulder-cuffing way of a helpful male companion? Was he telling me the truth? I didn't believe. This penis of mine had never let me down. But on the other hand, I knew from the beginning to be careful about what I asked. I stayed away from the gang assaults on beer-sodden ladies after football games at what was dignified with the name of party—vomit on the rug, giggle screams in the air, and face sits. I could see my impotence from miles away. I chose a thin-haired, bespectacled spook, walked the Gulf of Mexico beaches, and talked about William Carlos Williams. Then felt a small breast gently.

What is a penis anyway? The thing that was supposed to win with a longer stream in the back-alley stadium near my grandmother's house in Chicago? Stopping for a measurement, I was shortest in height and second in length, in a circle jerk conducted in a mosquito-infested near swamp during a vacation in Florida. At the height of my adolescent powers, I made a chubby, manic New York girl come seventeen times with a penis that felt like rubber and belonged to someone else. I wanted to send it home with her, she liked it so much.

But a later penis of mine felt like something else. Like my head, when it's angry. I'd stick it in the conversation like a battering ram. Into the productions of others, into the wars of words. The blood rushing through my body in hot readiness came out not in white and thick squirts but in a rain of phrases. The quick use of past history, remembered quotes, inconsistencies of previous argument, and all other possible evidence of fault, hypocrisy, dishonesty, intellectual incompetence, and questionable motivation.

We penis doctors, we psychiatrists, call all this stuff penis—even the erectile exhortations of a Southern Baptist minister.

Now, my penis is as delicate as I am, an easily turned-off thing. I'm squeamish about set and setting, and the mental quality of it all. Always cautious, I am now too paranoid to stick my penis into an unknown place. I have to see first if there are any teeth, or laughter. The flight has to start in the head. I have to know that my partner understands my miniaturizations: the use of catty cornered angles that stretch the sides like being big, my slow tantalization for sadistic deliciousness, my gentle bite that means violence. I'm as fragile as the hypothetical ladies in the technique books of the fifties. My clitoris must be addressed with reverence, vigor, and yet timely gentleness. My head needs even more care. The naked flesh doesn't arouse me as it did. It looks like risk. I feel my way head-first. Fearful of that moment, oh, so fearful of that moment when the wet, pink goody seems to be moving in feigned, fake hip shoving, and my flag comes down—before victory, before the battle. I can't fake it anymore and my orgasms produce no evidence. The abdominal nerves that are left are as confused about all this as I am. I'm birth-control safe and the danger is enormous.

Not so long ago, the crowd in Vegas took teasing delight in offering me a thirty-one-flavor variety pack of choices. I could have done The Lady and the Highwayman; the Hungry Little Girl and the Man with the Candy; Black Net Diapers and Red Ribbons for Two; Take That, You Nasty Man; and even She Was a Teenage Nun. My monk-shrink act bought me forbearance for my chastity and an acceptance of my eccentricities. Since I became a vegetarian the sight of a luscious and rare top sirloin fills me with nausea. But where can I turn?

The hairy ladies with sexual sweat smell, reading mystical magazines and doing yoga, I would have to examine after their shower and shave, in deafness for their gentle-mumble, dullingly vague, astrononsense from Thai sticks, coke, and Coors.

The New York Jewish intense and stylishly thin, cigaretting and amphetamining, marginal libbing with rapid-fire speech, producing a rat-a-tat rhetoric of a speeded dancer on the head of an amplified drum, talking and fucking all night with Quaaludes and without orgasm. Making for an endless climb over loose rocks and steep edges to get up to a mountaintop made of plastic and shaking from a rocking platform that the Disneyland company put down there near where the tickets are taken. There's the vision of my pitching forward colored by the blue-black anoxia of cardiac death, hearing just before I fall, "Next!"

In these years, my mole-blind instinctual intensity has moved under the aegis of thought. Feeling like a spiritual elevation, I know it's the sinking of the glands. My walking, idle obsessions with pink lips, hidden hairy nests, the thin ankles and long legs in the lobby of the Plaza; the tan-blond fullness on the beaches of California; the matter-of-fact, wooden-clog gait of the statuesque Scandinavians; the little flat behinds of the vivacious girls of Paris; the coy, disapproving hunks of white flesh, pink-cheeked, of London; the dark and protuberant firmness of a balloon in early inflation and soon to fan into soft obesity of the Italians—all have become a part of a quiet collection. My museum of erstwhile turgor. There's a delight in the new freedom from my passions, and a fear that whereas an erect penis meant life, its absence means death. Is the life-force that is so difficult to locate now the same energy that used to wake me up in the morning with an erection?

The temptation is to begin a new chase. Now not for the automatic movements of hips that bring an explosive release, but a desperate, breathless chase of life. My chase after the rabbit would really be a run from death, running into a new hole so that the black-clad hunter over my shoulder can't find his kill. Must I prove in this way that I'm still living? An up-sticking toughness that will make that collector of the used-up retreat?

I need someone to tell me about penises. But I can't ask. A crashing down of a personally held myth of super-competence is too much for me to pay. When people played doctor with me, I was always the doctor. But not now.

"I'll be up to see you again soon." Kapilloff rose slowly and patted me on the leg through the wall of the oxygen tent.

FOUR

A new patient joined us at midnight, was shocked out of fibrillation, and talked to his wife. An hour later his heart ran off and stopped. This time they cut a hole in his trachea, connected his lungs to a respirator, and started him up again.

Whomp! His body jerked on the hard bed like a shaken rag doll as they shocked his chest for him to begin. His gray-blue became pale pink. The rhythmic sound of the respirator was like air passing through clenched teeth. I watched between quiet white coats with the tingling horror of viewing a freeway accident. It was too late. The machinery, engaged in maintaining the body, heart, and lungs of a dead brain, bought time to break the news.

The bluebells, now among other well-wishing flowers, were wilted.

I was thirty-nine when my coronary arteries were used up. My heart fed me, they were to feed my heart and were clotted. The cardiologist spoke about changing my life-style. I didn't know what he meant. How can a middle-aged man understand that he must stop walking with a strange gait—when no one had mentioned it before? Hard-nosed, frightened, I demanded the data. With the nihilism of a medical scientist, I thought we were discussing a choice of decorations while nature took its course. My doctor listened with a knowing smile. All driven, Type-A

47

personalities feel that way. So I read a book and made a list. I lost forty pounds of overweight, gave up the chairmanship, stopped lecture tours—staying around the quiet work of my laboratories, took medicine to reduce my blood fats, and started to run. Was that what they meant by life-style?

My fear machine worked on. The specter of heart disease had made things worse. Locatable dangers grew vague and pervasive. Small messages from my body had sinister import. Dangerous information invoked more compulsive food stuffing, cigarette smoking, and agitated pushing for the imagined safety of power. I worked into the night, drank coffee all the time, and raced from death in fright-high craziness. Perverted security operations, called into play during times of danger—my whole life felt like danger—became my assassins. A killer of Western man is the attachment of his survival drives to self-destructive tics like cigarette smoking and overeating. How can one feel the fear of sudden death and not call out one's lifelong army of action? Must I lie here and be vulnerable? Can't I do *something*? My answer came from a most unexpected place. My life-style was how it felt. How I felt was my brain chemistry. My brain chemistry could be influenced, without the use of drugs. Why didn't I know this? Why hadn't I been taught?

The friends of my youth denigrated physical exercise. High-school athletes got drunk, wrecked cars, and got poor grades. They were exhibitionistic and crude. They had fun. We, the less physically gifted, chose weird intellectual girls, whose firm and willing bodies were hidden behind glasses and intellectual comprehension. We called football players dummies. The competitive theme in all athletic activity had ruined my relationship to my body in the same way that grades from the normal curve have destroyed people's feelings about their brains. In an era of World War II masculinity, physically little, music-practicing, night-*Decameron*-reading, funny talkers like me could dream themselves into West Point's backfield, but we always came out carrying the towels. I couldn't make the team. Getting into condition and not making the team was humiliating. So I didn't get into condition. I didn't even know what getting into condition meant.

I peeked into the winner's circle in golf a few times— the best athletes didn't go out for the game in those days. For one stretch of fourteen months I hit four hundred golf balls a day—every day. Such tenacity, from a hurt desperation for a high-school letter, led to mid-seventies shooting— with the efficiency of teaching a bear to juggle. Besides the lack of coordination, there was another problem with golf: how to make slow and rhythmic movements when screwed up tight for an explosion. Golf for people like me is like more practice for a heart attack. But as I remember now, there was a message that I missed. On days that I hit four hundred balls *and* played thirty-six holes in a hot summer sun, I noticed that the noisy and hyperactive crab claws on the slate floor of my brain grew quiet; a languorous contentment of the body. The physical peace of achievement without anything to hang on the wall. I should have realized that was important. But we inhabitants of oxygen tents are known for not hearing messages from our bodies until it's almost too late.

Then my back's full feeling, a bad electrocardiogram, a talk with my cardiologist, and reading about running. At the age of thirty-nine, I found my body.

I put on a green running suit and red Adidas shoes, looked in the mirror, and felt embarrassed. In these pretentious garments I envisioned myself representing Mars— I believed they would wear green in the Games. Remembering the warnings about sudden deaths in middle-aged men during Saturday-picnic sack races, I stopped three times to take my pulse. Bored, breathless, achy, and awkward, I persevered. The same stubborn deafness to body messages that killed became my strength. I'd turn my compulsiveness on itself. Each day a little longer. I ran fifty yards slowly and walked fifty yards briskly. Then a little more. The shadowy fullness in my back returned with too much optimism. I kept careful track of my enemy and as time passed I felt it retreat. Soon I could jog a mile and only nod to it in passing. Then farther. Within sixteen months I could go ten miles in a hundred minutes and had a resting pulse of 54. It was then that the secret that deprecating gym teachers had kept from me was revealed: being in condition is a drug for the mind.

The first thirty minutes are tough, old man. Creaks, twinges, pain, and stiffness. A counterpoint of breathless, painful self-depreciation. Like driving a mule. You ol' fart, you lazy fat ass, you brain-heavy jerk. Keep going! Challenged, I smile with pride and follow my orders. That's what professional football players call playing hurt. Maybe if I were bigger I could have done that, that macho thing in shoulder pads. The first thirty minutes hurt until the body gets the message that you're serious.

Thirty minutes out, and something lifts. Legs and arms become light and rhythmic. My snake brain is making the best of it. The fatigue goes away and feelings of power begin. I think I'll run twenty-five miles today. I'll double the size of the research grant request. I'll have that talk with the dean and tolerate no equivocating.

Then, sometime into the second hour comes the spooky time. Colors are bright and beautiful, water sparkles, clouds breathe, and my body, swimming, detaches from the earth. A loving contentment invades the basement of my mind, and thoughts bubble up without trails. I find the place I need to live if I'm going to live. The running literature says that if you run six miles a day for two months, you are addicted forever. I understand. A cosmic view and peace are located between six and ten miles of running. I've found it so everywhere. In Munich, running in the rain at five in the morning so I could lecture sanely at eight, I was stopped by a confused German policeman. It was in Oklahoma City at 104 degrees when I was bitten by a frightened dog. It was in Ann Arbor, buried in two feet of snow; outside coal-foggy

London; on the Hebrew University track, a block away from the Arab killings of Jews that morning; along the Seine in a Paris winter of 4 degrees, chased by barge watchdogs; in Central Park past torn women's garments scattered on the bridle path; at eight thousand feet in Aspen on a high-school track; embellished by manure smell along the farms of the Sacramento Valley; in the hot dryness of Palm Springs; in the hot wetness of Houston.

After the run I can't use my mind. It's empty. Then a filling begins. By afternoon I'm back into life with long and smooth energy, a quiet feeling of strength, the kind wisdom afforded those without fear, those detached yet full. The most delicious part is the night's sleep. Long an illusive, fickle dealer with me, Father Sandman now stands ready whenever *I* want. Maybe the greatest power of the second cycle is the capacity to decide when to fall asleep.

I told my cardiologist about all this. He said it was a change in my life-style.

Until relatively recently the only way to talk to the brain was with words. Using this language, words in— words out, the philosophers, psychologists, and psychiatrists built theories of brain function. It was a very tricky business in that the brain is so flexible, so able to come up with whatever is being sought, that the student never knows whether the data are the products of discovery or invention. Experienced behavioral scientists can, unknowingly, make a suitably controlled experiment come out any way they want. Like squirrels, whose nuts are stored for the winter, they are delighted to discover answers that they themselves have buried in the experimental design.

The discovery of electrical events as concomitants of neural activity led to the next form of dialogue with the brain: electricity in—electricity out. Equipped with ever more sophisticated computers to simplify the messages and discriminate them from noise, the neurophysiologists brought us pictures of the brain. This work is done by biologists whose metaphysic involves adaptation for survival. Groin talk. They gave us the lower, middle, and upper brain, described the middle brain's prepotence, and established the scientific basis of the domination of our era by the priests of the first cycle: Darwin, Freud, and Marx. And Vincent Lombardi.

The new era of brain chemical studies and the understanding of the actions of psychotropic drugs (chemical in—chemical out) have added new theoretical dimensions. Whereas the time required for an evolutionary change in the brain is eons, a potent chemical messenger can give one a new brain biology in a matter of minutes. Whereas the intellectual activity of the upper brain used to sound like light chatter by an ivory-tower commentator when compared to the flesh work of the middle brain, the upper brain's choice of one pill or another now gives this professor real power.

Is it possible that the dignity of choice, once promised by Aristotle, has been given to us at last in the form of chemicals? Is this a new era of upper-brain power? Are there now openings for second-cycle abstractionists in place of the concrete football philosophers? Will a culture emerge that is joyful in more than fighting and fucking? Will aging be less terrifying with the discovery of an ecstasy that doesn't require triumph? Can death be an ecstasy of the second cycle? As the data of neuroanatomy and neurophysiology harmonized with the first cycle's concerns, brain chemistry will be the biological science of reference for the second cycle. Upper-brain, second-cycle cosmologists are yet to emerge, though it is not beyond possibility that Timothy Leary, whose instructions to turn the upper brain on were met with harassment and jail, will be the era's first sacrificed saint and Julius Axelrod, who made fundamental contributions to brain chemical research, its first Nobelist.

We used the onion as an image of man's electrical brain. Man's chemical brain can be visualized as a bubbling pool of continually changing hue, tinted by pigments of feeling released from floating gland bags.

Red is the activation of alertness, fear, attacking, escaping, protecting, and mating. Yellow is the fearful inhibition of the actions of red. Blue stills the racket from external disruption and the ruminative noise that is its echo. White is the highness of euphoria and hope; black, depression and despair. Thoughts are floating glass figurines taking their shapes from the mold of perception and memory, their color from the pool. Colors change gradually, biased in the direction of the latest release. The blueness of quiet and the whiteness of high bring an aqua of awe. Red rage, purpling, muddies it. Some red assertiveness, yellowed by fear, may mean the orange of neurotic paralysis, or the orange light of appropriate caution. Can the blackened pool of the depressive transmit any color but itself? There is no hierarchical arrangement in this vision, no illusion of the objective and rational executive on high. All that there is, is in the soup. How much power in these hues? As much as lighting can change the feeling of a stage without moving any furniture.

Drugs control the valves of the gland bags. They influence the rates of release of the pigments of feeling. Amphetamine brings red and sometimes pink, if that brain's high white comes from winning. The quick, flashing prose of Tom Wolfe and the sacking of a quarterback are in the bag of red. Kerouac was on amphetamine when writing the red, restless prose of *On the Road*; on pot to make the cool blue sounds of *The Subterraneans*.

The brain has mechanisms to dampen its excitement. Runaway red is incompatible with sanity. Negative feedback loops are the theoretical device used to explain inhibitory control in electrical terms. In the chemical brain, the courage of red is bound to the release of fearsome yellow, which may outlive it. The late effect of alcohol is a good example of such long-lasting yellowing. At first, alcohol's release of red and white leads to the break-shy engagement of others, the activation of sexual approaches, the grandiloquence of silent, barstool planning. In *A Fan's Notes*, Frederick Exley's mind travels to Giant football stardom, to sexual exhaustion of virgins, to literary greatness. However, with every exultant red squirt there is the secretion of yellow—the inhibitory control of red wildness by sallow fear. When one gives up booze, the red-white glory goes quickly, the more slowly disappearing yellow speaks. Malcolm Lowry's life of dread. Exley's months of hiding on his mother's couch and in mental hospitals. Alcohol brings red relief but indentures more months of yellow. This mad work by the brain colorist is called alcoholism. Tranquilizers like Librium and Valium shut off the release of yellow until the pressure in the bag makes the valve leaky. More yellow is released than before. Is it possible that the antiyellow red of alcohol and amphetamine, and the antiyellow of the tranquilizers, by creating more cowardly yellow, are creating needs for themselves?

The red-yellow polarity in the chemical brain is as much a matrix for conflict as the electrical argument in the middle brain about individual versus species survival: fearful retreat versus creative emergence. Whitman's ". . . coming from under" and Bellow's Augie March were triumphs of red over the yellow of their literary pasts that one could argue were fueled by naturally occurring changes in brain chemistry. Can this be achieved with drugs? Recent advances in brain chemistry have given us two new groups of compounds which, though far from predictably effective, suggest possibilities. Each produces a different form of detachment. One detaches the red-bag mechanism from fear, so reddening produces no yellow. The other leads to fresh energy without the use of red at all.

The antidepressant drugs were a lifesaving discovery. Black pools, hereditary in origin, blot out the experience of life and are resistant to changing their color with talk. Until the antidepressant drugs clear the vision, other colors can't be seen. Another, recently discovered, effect of the antidepressants is their gradual release of red without the production of yellow. These drugs detach assertion from trepidation. Energizing red brings no yellow of disapproval. The chemical detachment of red from the yellow mechanism may result in people with more social mobility, less sensitivity to criticism, more psychological toughness. It gives people with inborn depressive and fearful sensitivity a chance to lead—a new breed of executive. One who brings more empathy into the hard business of ruling.

The other group of detachment drugs functions independently of the culturally resonant red and yellow systems, projecting human feeling into another realm. The euphorohallucinogens release blue-white for weeks. Some speculate, permanently. Turning the pool into diamond glitter, producing an ecstasy that alienates and a spectacle that is never forgotten. Blue-white is the freedom of something new; it changes the colors of living. Not fighting, not fearing, not fucking, not winning—it nonetheless gives ecstasy. Not the ecstasy of triumph but of change, of discovery, of insight, of escape from both red and yellow, of joyful aging and good death. An ecstasy that is available, without drugs, in the second cycle to those who can abandon their addiction to the kidney-crunching wars of survival; to those who can give up the gods of football. Chemical messengers have taught us of these pathways into the spiritual and intellectual playground of the upper brain, freeing our insights and knowledge from imprisonment in the habitual. The religions of the East recommend decades of meditation, renunciation, and exercise to find this path which to impatient Westerners can be revealed through the suffrage of a chemical.

One evening near Gaya in northeast India, south of the now-named town of Patna, Gautama sat under the bo tree. He was nearing the end of a six-year search for a force that would take him from the things that were to what they were to become. As was his practice for hours each day, he was engaged in meditation, ever deepening as the night progressed. The bo tree encouraged him with its blossoms, raining them down on him through that moon-filled May night. As the morning star made its appearance in the East, his mind shook free from the last of its worldly attachments, and then, as Clarence Hamilton describes it in *Buddhism: A Religion of Infinite Compassion,* ". . . ten thousand galaxies shuddered in awe as lotuses bloomed on every tree, turning the entire universe into a bouquet of flowers . . ." Are you a god? the people asked. An angel? A saint? No, he replied. Then what are you? *I am awake,* was his answer. That's what Buddha means, to be awake, free from the boring sleep of everyday existence, alive! The blue-white, revealed detachment from the mundane, from the reds and yellows of the world, from the fearful sweat of Darwin, Freud, and Marx, from hate, from winning and losing. Feeling this way makes one kindly. Ecstatic detachment brings compassion. It's in the brain. I know it. What's more, the rumors of its presence have been around for too many centuries to doubt it.

There are a number of chemical messengers for the brain that are not drugs. A moderate reduction in the usual intake of food leads to more red during the day and less sleep at night. The same kind of increase in red results from a purposeful reduction in sleep time. The combination of moderate sleep loss and diet produces the alert hyperactivity of a small dose of amphetamine and an antidepressant effect. This red response comes from teasing the brain about survival.

Daily exercise, running thirty minutes or more, swimming actively for an hour, brings a light red, free of yellow (research has suggested that this may work like the antidepressant drugs), an antiblack effect, and, for those with the available pathways, some blue. With more massive effort the blue can become white. Runners get tougher— more confident of their strength and worth. Long runners get mystical.

Regular times of psychological retreat, sensory isolation or meditation, bring blue and sometimes blue-white. Thoughts rise to the mind not in a linear, problem-solving, threat-driven mode, but as bubbles to the surface from we know not where. New insights, creative images, answers, and calm knowledge come like gifts from an unharassed brain. Toynbee says that the blue-white of those moments, from a withdrawal and a return, account for most of the creativity in history.

Cold, heat, music, overwhelming beauty, simplicity and repetitiveness in daily routine, hypnosis, muscle-relaxation training, and short periods of swamping psychological overload are all powerful mutators of the color pool. The specific effects of each, like the actions of drugs, are dependent on the response characteristics of the pool, the gland bags, and the valves of each individual brain. Talk seems ineffective for doing fundamental color work. It may, however, change the color of the lenses in the spectacles of the observer.

FIVE

A bored orderly wheeled a body out of the unit this morning before sunrise. I had been sleeping when they covered his future with a sheet. My diagnosis, reversible or permanent, had not been decided. So far, two companions at this border station had crossed over.

Nights weren't easy. Drug ups were shorter and followed by flat and restless downs. Night vision dim and without strong powers of smell, man's eyes and brain, built for daylight danger, feel vulnerable in the dark. How does one tell the blinded brain to surrender its alertness in the presence of enemies? Lie still as toes curl and hands clench for climbing trees out of danger. Frightened, breathe rhythmically in the lullaby beat of Mother's heart, hoping for a hypnosis to still the silent screams of fight-ready muscles.

Last night my sons visited me as I lay between the two worlds: an unknown darkness in one direction, frightened witnesses in the other. I looked back at their faces, unable to help.

None of us Western car racers has been taught to meditate on wrecks. We excuse this cowardice as protection from thoughts we fear may provoke. We see death with a quick glance, throw salt over our shoulder, and talk beside the point. We've separated dying from living, using hospitals, extended care facilities, and one-stop mortuaries. Professional football coaches will not allow injured players to sit on the bench to remind the combatants. It's all because we know that few pieces of knowledge can change brain function as much as the acceptance of our mortality. More than a guaranteed income, the inevitability of death takes energy out of the fantasied reward in our mad competition for power.

Like other occasions of strong emotion in childhood, first meetings with death are remembered. Color-pool fear, middle-brain defense, and upper-brain philosophy join to etch permanent pictures. These create the symbolic meaning of the event. Like letters in wet cement, this word carving is difficult to change. A child who loses his leg after ten experiences a phantom limb. The mind's shape of the body, fat or thin, is learned between twelve and fifteen and never changes, no matter what the later reality. Foreign language cannot be learned as a language of thought after the middle teens. The forbidding silence that children experienced in the past from questions concerning sex they now receive about death. It's the new pornography. The potential for calm beauty in dying has only recently been creeping into our consciousness via television portraits of the dying elderly and a new genre of books for children. It's too late for me.

I was spending my seventh summer with my grandparents on the near North Side of Chicago, when one afternoon I asked about a neighbor who filled my past visits with potato pancakes and applesauce. They said she had gone away. The quick movement of their eyes to the floor shut off questions and produced a wave of abdominal fear. I persisted. Where was she? Everywhere and nowhere; eyes down again. Alone in my unknowing, their fatalistic sadness seemed like the surrender of the aged. I wanted to know the rules of battle and I would get ready.

They told me to pray and do good works. Puzzled, I wasn't going to take any chances. I promised obedience and goodness. In prayer, I negotiated for the welfare of my loved ones, an ever-lengthening list of family and friends. I added my name to the bottom of the list lest He think I was selfish. Hard work was emphasized by my grandfather. It was all so mysterious.

They took me along on their weekly trips to the cemetery. The photographs on some of the stones were eerie—where were those people? My grandfather told me that the real selves of the people, their souls, weren't under the rocks. I asked him what we were visiting. He consulted my grandmother in a fast Yiddish that I couldn't follow, and their joint statement on the matter was that we were paying our respects. To whom or for what was never clarified.

Out came the rituals of primitive man. If you step on a crack you break your mother's back. I never opened an umbrella in the house. Don't come back into the house for forgotten items; my grandmother insisted that she get them. My days were spent bargaining with an unseen and voiceless force. I learned to give up pleasure for the safe feeling of being deprived. Joy became dangerous. I hoarded sacrifice to pay off death's bagman.

Praying turned out to be complicated. My grandfather told me that people prayed about death in a synagogue. My parents had stopped going, and I knew little about it. I went with him on Saturdays to learn. He wore a white skullcap and a prayer shawl with fringes, and we walked; the Sabbath rules required it. Old men were crowded into a small room chanting incomprehensible Hebrew. It sounded grim. Cries of disappointment and anguish. Some standing, some sitting, some nodding, some shaking, each man listed his complaints. These experts on death were hard at work in minor keys. It sounded as though they were all in trouble.

Though the metaphysic of death wasn't clarified at my grandparents' house, I did learn how love and wisdom together reduce fear. Their early expressions sank deep:

Never trade horseshit for cowshit.

All the world rotates on the head of a penis.

She has more sense between her legs than his mother has on her shoulders.

If I knew how to read and write, I would be a janitor.

An understanding mate is a messenger from God.

They were all said in Yiddish, which I could never pass on a language exam, but it still talks to my innards like no other sound. I got a message about humanism, man's kindness to man, that serves as transcendence in place of a savior. The Jewish religion is about living. When it comes to death, Jews show the same kind of crankiness with which they deal with any interference.

Saturday's music of Hasidic intensity was followed by the quiet of Sunday morning's more secular rite: eating. I took walks with my grandfather to the delicatessens on Kedzie Street. The memory of the tastes and smells of those Jewish cardiovascular poisons (in your mouth for thirty seconds and on your coronary arteries for the rest of your life) bring warm feelings. Herring, bagels (egg, onion, water, and rye), cream cheese, smoked whitefish, lox, onion rolls, tomatoes, cheddar cheese for the soft omelet, and some halvah to nibble on the way. I walked with my hand in his, enjoying the stories of his escape from Russia. Real cowboy stuff. Blood on the whips of the cossacks dripping on the snow, deaths by the dozens in train stations. I joined him in thanking God that he made it. He taught me a pride in my forebears, about the tenacity of the breed. Two years work in the sweatshops of Chicago's garment industry to pay for his wife's and my mother's passage. Fourteen hours a day and six days a week of piecework. Sleeping in a borrowed room and eating as little as possible. Saving the ticket money in a coffee can. He opened a fruit store, and he, his wife, and daughter lived in back, saving money for their first home. Working, building, saving, and caring, this little man put generations of us into business.

His eyes crinkled in laughter about once-difficult times. The fruit store went broke three times in four years before he found that his wife had been skimming. She put thousands of dollars in a sock under the bed, a *knippel*. His second daughter died in childhood. He told me that even at such times, he didn't doubt the wisdom of God. Years later, when I sought the source of my manhood, my mind went to this man. I have felt his quiet and resolute strength coursing through me in times of difficulty—not the flamboyant barks of a frightened small dog, my father's style. Football coaches say that making it happen costs the body; my grandfather helped teach me to pay it. Through hypertension, struggles, and strokes, his kind and reasonable voice never changed. Though he didn't believe in a literal afterlife, he gave me a glimpse of something. It came from what you have done for others. For him, it was being the back-bridge upon which his family crossed the water to a new life. I asked about a heaven of joy, and he spoke of work to be done. I compared the Disneyland paradise of my friends with the talk of my grandfather and decided that when it came to giving out heavens, the Jews were short-changed. But his peaceful readiness when he turned his face to meet death remains unforgettable.

I had nightmares after returning home from Chicago. Several nights, screaming, I woke my parents. I practiced my piano longer, my room was clean without my mother's nagging. When things were in place and work was all done, I felt better. The calming influence of orderly work. I asked and was sent to Sunday school. Its mix of history, ethnic practices, and chauvinism got me ready to face prejudice and persecution, but not death. I talked about it to my teachers and got the impression it wasn't in the curriculum. Ashamed to speak about my fears with anyone, I found my way into the bizarre thoughts of a recluse. I grew afraid to sleep.

Ashamed or not, it was time to talk to my father. Could one influence the Fates? We read Robert Blatchford's *Not Guilty* together. Through the writings of this early twentieth-century criminologist, I learned that what one did was a product of heredity and environment—not choice. To this day I gather the neurological evidence. I remember both a relief from the worrisome responsibility of touching every crack and a new horror at my helplessness.

What would protect me from the enemies in the bushes, sexual kidnappers in slowly moving cars, cossacks with whips in the shadows? Practicing my music and getting all A's except in citizenship (I talked too much) didn't change the dark shapes outside my bedroom window, the creeping edge of the other world that began at the border of ours. I asked my father to take me to synagogue. My father, an intellectual and agnostic man, said that there was no mystical power in organized religion, only man power. He told me that I made up the fears; he explained the mechanism of projection. I argued that he had misread the cosmos, that there was a spirit of death upon the land. If that wasn't so, why did evil men entice Pinocchio away from his father? Why would Humpty Dumpty have a skull fracture? Why was Dorothy almost killed by a witch? Long John Silver threatened the boy with dismemberment and death. If these were the products of my head, why were they everywhere? He sighed in frustration and planned my treatment.

He would drive me a mile away from the house on a moonless night in our dimly lit suburban neighborhood and I was to walk around a block and count the houses. He'd wait in the car. It sounded simple, and the full import didn't hit me until dinnertime. I couldn't eat. In an anxious fog, I kept my eyes slightly closed to soften the starkness of things. A nail-biting, teeth-grinding nausea. My muddled head clung to meaningless ritual: counting the blue dots on the tablecloth with my eyes; arranging salad carrots in a triangle. Even murderers don't have to walk their last mile alone in the dark. I thought about killing him. But then I would have no father.

I started, sauntering in slow dignity. He would see that the treatment was unnecessary. One house, two houses, three houses. It felt fine! Then I began to wonder why it felt fine, and the worry started—as if the worry itself were a protection. I walked faster. The outlines of the low evergreens gave me the most trouble; people could be hidden in their shadows. A long, trunked tree served as respite; I could check both sides casually. My own fast walking became a trigger for fear. The shadow behind the wheel of a parked car was the murderer with a knife in the evening news. Two more houses and I began to run. Dark shapes were denizens from my museum of fears: scientific tortures, big beater-uppers, robbers, sex perverts with enema bags. I ran faster, chased by the movies: Arabs on camels with curved swords; English polo players with mace and chains; black knights with lances; German spies from a submarine; Japanese kamikaze pilots; masked men from an unnamed island. I got more breathless; each gasp brought a sticking pain in my side. I slowed down as I approached the car, but my breathing gave me away. I opened the car door quickly, gasping, comforted by the smell of his cigar. I was safe. Ashamed.

"How many did you count?" He looked straight ahead, sternly, as he started the motor.

"Sixteen or eighteen. I got mixed up." I could hardly talk over the breathlessness and pain.

"Wrong. There're twenty-one. You were too scared to count." He shook his head slowly in disapproving disbelief as we pulled away from the curb. I was too worn out to bleed for him anymore. God damn it, I tried. Shit on him. Maybe he was right. The bastard. Why was it always this way with him? Killing me while helping? But maybe he was trying to make me strong. I stayed as silent as my breathing would allow.

"We're going to do it over and over until you can stay calm enough to count." He puffed on his cigar, driving slowly back to the house.

The anticipation was more than I could bear. There was no dignity left; I could only plead. "Dad, I'm scared. The story on the radio about those kids killed by that man with the knife. They haven't caught him yet." I was crying in breathless sobs. His expression didn't change. Lombardi would call it toughening. I see it now as angry shame about his own fears.

"No son of mine is going to grow up and be a coward. Afraid of the dark at eight? Tomorrow we begin again."

We drove up the driveway in silence. My feelings kept changing. An immediate relief from danger. Shame. Rage. Second thoughts about his motives; it was, after all, for my own good. Lots of fathers wouldn't even bother. Dread about more to come. I crept upstairs into my bedroom, red-faced, sweaty, tears still running, right side feeling as though a knife were in deep. I didn't want my mother to see me like this. I'll do it, just wait. I'd show the son of a bitch. But at the same time, I promised that I would never do this to a son of mine. No matter how much good it was supposed to do.

There was so much power in my relationship to my father. Everything was strong. Love, hate, fear, and need. He talked about his frustrated wish to direct movies. He pointed it at me. Total control of my miniworld; he spared no production costs. He was Zanuck, Svengali, and Mussolini. He made his charge look great and his trains run on time. I was a fearless creator, obedient to his maker. A manufactured genius. In his pride of authorship, I was assigned papers and orchestrations to write; piano, saxophone, clarinet, and tap dancing to practice; science, history, biography, economics, and psychology to read. Look up the words you don't understand. He hired tutors in everything from high jumping to Yiddish. With a gun in my back, only a forward race to competence afforded safety. The quid pro quo was signs of accomplishment in exchange for an umbrella of security from the dangers he created. He told his friends what I was doing and I enjoyed the eroticism of specialness.

"This is my moment," Tubby the Tuba's triumphant song, came from hard work and risk. A spotlight's kiss for skydiving perfectly. A chair near god came to him who had guts and perfectionistic compulsion. He was my first religion, a mustached shaman who made demands, threatened, and promised safety. Like all ex-believers, my views about childhood belief are probably distorted. I know it taught me to hang on hard, wrench my guts, and pay the price. He sold me a commitment to middle-brain values.

"Before you go to sleep, I want you to make a list of the things you're afraid of. Tomorrow, before you count the houses, we'll discuss them. But remember, talk is all right, but action is the only answer to fear."

I slept with my head under the covers. Peering out from that cave, the shadows on the ceiling were people. The wind through the leaves was them whispering. I was fortified by my bedside arsenal: two toy rifles, three baseball bats, and a loaded cap pistol. At first Mother put away my things in the morning. Finally she helped me arrange them neatly.

The moments just before falling asleep were the scariest. Shadowy figures got solid. I heard my thoughts coming from a dark corner. Once I heard my mother scream as though she were being killed. A cricket outside my window told his fellow spacemen that this was the place to land. My mother interrupted my loud dreams with calm explanation; my father, with disgust.

Just before going to sleep I thought about death. I'd rehearse it. Was it like not feeling anymore? Like sleeping when you didn't know you were? Like not being born yet?

A helpful perspective came from an unexpected place, Disney's *Fantasia*. The enormous extension of time backward into the prehistoric world gave me my first feelings for infinity. Man—I—was a speck on the time line of living things. It was reassuring. I know that good feeling now, and it's a treatment for the dying. I stood by the Gulf in Sarasota, Florida, in the moonlight and saw an endless progression of waves. I was nothing, an ephemeral blip. Buddha says there's a treatment for fear in the shrinking of the *I*. Moonlit waves and dinosaurs helped. Wandering a redwood forest in northern California, I saw a circular, continuous process. The trees were in all gen-

erations: tall, vigorous adults; short adolescents; children
with thin green limbs; dead trunks lying on the ground,
defeated in heroic battle with lightning, age, and rot. The
essential stuff, carbon and nitrogen, cycled endlessly. Why
invent a termination and call it death?

From my father's treatment I learned to keep quiet
about fear. To be gruff about it. Tough about it. Lie
about it. But in my privacy I researched. I read everything
I could find. Astronomy for space, biology for time, philosophy for belief, psychology for myth. I remember spending evenings with a rabbi named Joshua Loth Liebman
who promised me *Peace of Mind.* One day I thought I'd
found it: a physiological psychology text that said feelings
were bumps on the head—it was a very old book, but it
promised the most. Fear in the brain, like temperature in
a house, might be regulatable, using the products of science. I've been working at that job.

When I was ten a new fear came into our house. The
family took long walks, me up ahead, my father and
mother behind. My parents, serious, sad, talked quietly;
my mother cried. Our mealtime's boisterous conversations
stopped. My father ate little and didn't speak at all.

My mother and I flew to Chicago and waited for my
father to join us at my grandmother's. Free from his
supervision, I played my favorite game: I was a medical
researcher working on a new cure, using salt, pepper,
spices, bicarbonate of soda, fruit concentrates, vinegar,
and tea in my grandmother's kitchen. I spilled bubbles
and colors all over the floor. Without my mother's "Wait
until your father gets home," I was wild and free. Creative.

One morning I turned my grandparents' big bed into
a trampoline, bouncing to the rhythm of my mother's
shouts. A joyful release and a peculiar excitement.

Suddenly my father was in the doorway. I almost
fainted. I jumped quickly off the bed and stood frozen in
the glare of his angry brown beams.

"What in the hell are you doing? Is this the way you
honor my trust?"

"I . . . I . . . I . . ."

"My son. The one I count on. Destroying instead of helping!"

"I didn't . . . I can't . . . You see . . ." I couldn't talk.

"Do you know why we're here? Do you have some idea about what's going on?"

I shook my head.

"We weren't going to tell you, but now I must. You can see for yourself what you've done." There was a sudden softening of his voice.

"They've discovered that I have cancer of the eye. My left eye. We're here so I can go to a special doctor and have it removed. It may be too late." He spoke slowly. I saw a tear coming down his cheek.

That moment of horror. A shudder with goose bumps. Self-disgust, hatred. I had destroyed my father's eye. Maybe my father.

"I didn't know . . . I mean . . . no one told me . . . I just thought we were here visiting. If only I had known . . ."

"I hope you never forget. I may live a few more months or years. But I hope you never forget."

I shuddered again. When I think about it I shudder now. A part of me went down into a dark cellar for father killers where it stays to this day. I sometimes think that some of the darker aspects of my own thoughts of death, my difficulty with the anger of my sons and students, comes from the anticipation of the arrival of a score-settling event. Sons sitting around a table eating the flesh of their father was Freud's *Totem and Taboo.* Death visited my left testicle and my father's left eye.

Both of us lived to continue our romance.

SIX

Professors are inclined to embellish. Making things fancy keeps the students' attention and confirms us in our specialness. We also owe them the truth. Tense between these two goals, we method actors of the mind doubt even the most heartfelt of our statements. Was that a flash of insight or the klieg lights hitting my tap-dancing shoes?

I spend hours examining my baubles for fraud. When a gem of unquestionable validity appears, it brings relief, promising an excited moment of exposition without someone outside to keep the motor running; when the speculations of research turn into clinical fact.

Cancer was concepts: cells not stopping their reproductive ways, chains of darkly straining corpuscles intruding, a riotous disorganization of chemical affairs. Then, as a student, one day I saw it. A woman, blinded by fears, ignored a breast lump for two years—the smell and the chest rot were cancer.

Schizophrenia was a confused scrabble for me; a terrified driver with a stuck gas pedal on downtown streets; slippage between the data accrual and management systems; a hallucinogenic, drug-seeping tumor of the frontal lobe. Then I saw a Jesus Christ stab himself and a wax statue stick girl starve.

Freud, Abraham, and Reich, early practitioners of the psychoanalytic arts, found that when nervous people

71

were asked to lie down on couches in the offices of stern-looking European physicians and told to say anything that came into their minds—so much more stress than any well person should have had to handle—they reacted with what were called resistances. It was soon noted that the style of the patient's battle for survival in these strange, dark, and quiet sanctums was an exaggerated expression of his individuality in everyday life, traits gathered like weapons to deal with the threat. These features of the patient's self, called *character*, stood out more than the symptoms that brought him to the ritual exorcism in the first place. As might be predicted, there were a limited number of defensive operations; each person was consistent in his style. Physicians turned these behavioral arrays into diagnoses. Each patient was assigned an adjectival disease: hysterical, obsessive-compulsive, depressive, schizoid, hypomanic, immature, and inadequate. Everyone had one. A superficial reading of the early literature suggests that health is only an abstraction since it consists of the absence of *any* personality. Later workers with more constructive biases have renamed these clusters of traits *coping styles*. After my fourteen-year-old thought about my eccentricities, he concluded, "I figure it's not whether you're crazy or not, but whether you can make a living at it."

A pure character typology is a professional card trick. A patient can be labeled within fifteen minutes of meeting; but when I know him better the labels pile up, their margins get blurred, and the diagnostic litany disappears. A hypomanic may be a hysteric who manifests compulsive traits. The obsessive-compulsive is schizoid and depressed except when in Las Vegas. With few exceptions, I never found the pure types of Reich's *Character Analysis* until I began my work with NFL football players. These men are the tall clinical truths of personality typology.

It was a bizarre assignment, even for a psychiatrist. I was to live and work with a professional football team to find psychological factors that might be useful predictors of a player's success in the NFL. Every year a pool of five thousand college seniors become eligible for the draft. Superficial research reduces this number to eight hundred. Scouts, using repeated visits to each college, interviews with coaches and fellow players, and examinations of game films, winnow the number to five hundred. After the draft and two or three years of shuffling, there are a hundred left. Who are they? The physical facts—time in the forty, quickness, bench-press capacity, height and weight, and indicators of intelligence and coordination—cannot dictate the final discriminations. The last set of decisions is intuitive, idiosyncratic, even political. The words used are *toughness, hunger, ready to play*, and *good attitude*. Scouts sound as vague as diagnostic psychiatrists.

Three years of research led to a book, *The Nightmare Season*, and the finding that those whose personalities fit their positions, make it. Misfits or those without strong personality definition don't, no matter how great their athletic talent. The stereotypes are well demarcated. The game, a threat to life and livelihood, a fight for territory by a tribal family, and fighting-before-fucking of primordial man, demanded the expression of character as well as motoric skills. In football, as in life, there's so little time to think.

Members of the offensive team love structure and fight to defend it. More disciplined than the defensive team, they protect the status quo. They desire long practices and want restrictive rules. The offensive linemen's form of territorial aggression is stubborn immobility. Conservative in life-style and politics, they become bankers and Republicans. Color is added to the offensive team through the selfish-actor wide receiver, whom the rest of the offensive team resents for his exhibitionism, and the flanker-running back, whose arrogant trickiness makes him a more likely companion for like-minded members of the defensive squad.

The defensive team despises structure and works to destroy it. Defensive linemen rage joyfully against the rules, despise practice, and attack before thinking. The linebacker is more ambivalent about his aggression. He's been a class president and cleaned out a bar when someone insulted his girlfriend. Most fiercely territorial of all football players, he struggles for meaning; he guards the ground for his children. The defensive back is a depressed loner. Cheated out of glamour, he wreaks his revenge on the center of the spotlight, the wide receiver. The quarterback walks on water, not subject to the rules of ordinary men; some feel their arrogance is a human right; some are appointed by God.

Character in this context is a specialized function, each individual type serving general tribal good. Character holds us; we hold it. Surrendering it, detaching from it, is disappearing. Changing it without major neurobiological alteration may be fantasy. Beethoven's changing musical style, from Mozart to the Ninth, a major shift in character, was facilitated by the brain-sculpting spirochete of syphilis. Could it have been LSD in their frontal lobes that enabled the Beatles to escape from *Rubber Soul* to the *Magical Mystery Tour?* Did Philip Roth's shift from a five-year effort to please a finicky lady English professor in *When She Was Good* to the libidinal splat of Portnoy come from the freedom afforded by the chemical mania after the death of his wife? Was this same molecular muse the goad of Bellow's *The Adventures of Augie March,* Berryman's *Homage to Mistress Bradstreet,* or Hart Crane's *The Bridge?* Moving the self to another place requires exercises of the spirit like readying oneself to die. It feels as dangerous in contemplation; it looks like black emptiness out the door. The characterological self, one's territory, is difficult to leave. It requires the detachment of death.

We never notice our character when things run smoothly. We become aware of it when things go bad, notified by the noise made by the rubbing of people's incompatible parts. Lying to an offensive lineman is diplomacy to a wide receiver. Discipline that generates resentment in a defensive end brings security to a center. A blind-rage attack on the advancing enemy by a linebacker is unnecessary roughness for an offensive guard. "Fuck you!" to a southern Italian brings a face full of saliva and garlic bread for a few minutes, a hug, and then wine and dancing for hours. The same message delivered to a Scandinavian means being stalked by a blond rifleman for thirty years. In real-life pairs, it's in the examination of the pain of these differences that the roads to individual slavery or freedom become specified.

My serum enzymes have normalized, and I'm out from under the tent. The doctors' talk is getting optimistic.

My ex-wife sat today and looked at me with sad eyes. Of our twenty-two years, twelve were on the way up, and ten were coming down. At the beginning, stuck together like frightened new orphans at eighteen, we were going to be psychiatrist, psychologist, brain scientist, mother, father, leader, revolutionary—achieving everlasting safety by pleasing all the superparents and gods. Stuck, intertwined—libidinal glue worked wonders to bind together the stubbornly immobile offensive guard (she) and the ambivalently aggressive linebacker (I)—we mounted an attack on the world. Both running frightened, we used our relationship as we did our cars—hard, distractedly, and without service stops. It was enough for a long time. Through the terrors of our graduate work (she in psychology, I in medicine), through the rage at my Jewish and moneyed family's niggardly response to my early marriage (my father's requirement of primacy in affection was violated), through the financial panic of just starting out, through two young children, we made it. We started together so young and with so much capacity to make simple feelings complex that our melted-together intimacy became too intricate. Its cracks were difficult to discover and impossible to fix. Once-expedient and temporary arrangements achieved statutory permanence without a thought-through rationale.

There was also a clash of myths. The message from my father that manhood was the tender and protective enslavement of one's female, linebacker's talk, mixed poorly with her family's story of weak, unstable, or sickly men whose helplessness trapped great women, a zone block held stubbornly by my offensive-guard wife. Her extraordinarily high intelligence, her multiple scholarship awards, her participation in 1951 consciousness-raising groups with a few similarly gifted and fearful Stanford women—now that her progress through graduate school was slowed by a family—all went toward the creation of a pot of frustration and rancor that would age and fester under two boys' dirty diapers like a buried Vietnamese stew. She had a right to be a person too, and a half-psychologist, half-mother wasn't a whole person. We both in our ways were struggling to grow past the promise of lifelong security that comes with wingless slavery—tracts from the Depression propaganda of our youth.

The contract was broken during year twelve. I got cancer of the testicle, became suicidally depressed, then manic, and after a devoted monogamy that had lasted the whole time of our long relationship, I had my first affair: with the professor of nursing named Carole. We until then sat like mommy and daddy gods on the high seat of the belief that we were the only ones who could fulfill each other. An exclusive religion, a fragile religion, it required an isolation from the rest of the world. It fed the rich feeling of exclusivity to our egos, and filled in the screaming triumphs of our genitals with a thick, family feeling. Like getting high on Pablum. It felt good, and it was good for us too: a perfect dish for those to whom guilt isn't spice but poison.

Her terrors about my death became focused on the other woman and turned into a clawing rage. I didn't see Carole again. I groveled. Then stormed. She stayed distant with hurt pride, ran briefly, courting in-kind revenge, fucked me to faintness, and cried unconsolably. It's a clichéd story that you can read every month in *Cosmopolitan* or *Ms.*, depending on your politics. If a linebacker and an offensive lineman get too tangled for either to walk, their characterological inflexibilities prevent either repair or easy escape. To fix it, they would both have to leave their bodies, detach from the selves that they knew, in hopes that, once freed, they could fly together again in a new way. Neither of us knew how to do it.

I used to be one who worried about scratches on my automobile, whether someone had moved something on my desk, and got irritated with anyone who borrowed one of my fetish pens. Such fussiness goes with a person who has not known real pain.

That all changed for me one morning in the June of 1965 when I awoke to a new world. In the shower before six to get to my early morning ward rounds, reaching down to scratch myself with a gesture as old as the apes, the tip of my fourth finger hit a hard place on the top of my left testicle. Still sleepy, I thought, I hoped, I had imagined it. But it was there for every finger. First a pang, then a shudder. A cold computer voice recited a textbook.

Cancer of the testicle, the most likely possibility, occurs between the ages of fifteen and thirty-five and is fatal in two years. Some types are always fatal; others have higher survival rates. Treatment recommendations differ. The British recommend the removal of the testicle and a rain dance. The Americans go for broke with a radical node dissection, chemotherapy, and radiation. The operation results in the loss of ejaculation, and in some cases erectile potency. Emotionally stunned, my head clicked through the probabilities like a train hitting cross rails in a tunnel. The university surgeons, wanting a save at any price, would come after me with all their instruments. I imagined asking Mary to bring me a vial of morphine and a .45 pistol—to keep away my well-wishing friends.

The vise of fear loosened a little under the hot shower and I surveyed the future. I would never see my sons, ages ten and four, grow up. The insurance was probably enough. The next man, that would be critical. Mary, beautiful, warm, and bright, would bring another one

quickly. I played death scenes that were fearful and cling-
ing, but to no avail. It was then that I made a basic discovery about dying: It separates. It detaches. It alienates.
I was alone. Really alone. Pretend otherwise, everyone
else can stay, you have to go. They love, cry, send good
wishes, and wave, but you go through that door by yourself. The social noises that hide man's aloneness are bogus.
I learned of the enormous distance between people, even
if they are close. The withdrawal into my own orgasm
was the only comparable solitariness I had known—and I
had been ashamed of the selfishness of it. Dying, like
ecstasy, is a solitary experience. Much of my giving was
predicated on the promise that I would never be left alone.
I was cheated. I had been alone all along! I overpaid my
taxes, God damn it, and they owe me!

The discovery of the space between me and the others
made another space, one between the me that was talking
and the me that was thinking. Being was divided into social talk and bitter, internal diatribe. My sons' voices became distant sounds; my answer, a puppet voice put out
there for them to hear, my mind making grotesque caricatures. Was an ugly world easier to leave?

Mary joined us at breakfast. This was her last day
for running subjects. Soon she would have a Ph.D. with
distinction from her research about thinking styles. Don
told us about his friend, the rabbi's son, who blew up a
mailbox with large firecrackers. Little Ross, smiling, didn't
stop eating long enough to talk. From my mountaintop I
saw them. Sniffing and wiping my eyes in a spring attack
of allergy, I hid my tears long enough to get to the car.

Now came the struggle to call the doctor, the chief of
urology. I couldn't do it. Testicular cancer, highly ma-
lignant, went to the lungs quickly. In those days, that
meant it was over. Every minute counted—and didn't
count at all. Give up now, hide in the depression, don't
take a chance with losing, surrender. Or take the high
road. Pretend it didn't happen. Focus a narrow beam of
attention on work, as in childhood, shut out the noise of

parental death struggles with a book. At a desk in the corner of my laboratory I began to design a new procedure for the assay of urinary adrenaline. I kept busy up to the very moment my ward rounds began. Feel the body move and get things done; nothing could be wrong with this body, watch it do.

In my mind were wasted and dying bodies. Thin, white, weak, sad, smiling. Later, the metal dissection tables of the morgue. Formaldehyde and white coats, a bucket of guts and the liver. See the white spots of metastatic cancer. If I had started early enough, long before now, such thoughts could have been a form of prayer. An Eastern sect, knowing that the sudden confrontations with death bring carnage to the living, meditates on corpses in various states of decay: the meditation for the blue-white limp one; another for a white rigid one; a third for one that is gaseous and bloated; a fourth for one with the sweet smell of bacterial rot. Practice for dropping your body.

I positioned my head for a straight look. I had seen four young men die of my illness. When I was an intern, a young physician was hospitalized on my service with a mysteriously enlarged lymph node in his neck. Consultants searched him with hands, X rays, and chemical tests. Nothing. I did one more physical exam and found the hard place on his testicle. He was dead in four months. I must go to the phone and call the doctor. Trust him. I couldn't.

After an afternoon lecture to the medical students, I went to my office to see patients. A silent, dark office with a couch and a desk. As I remained immobile and listened to their free associations, the voices floated away. Yesterday's important insight was today's trivia. My deny-and-do defense didn't work in that sanctuary. The corners of my office filled with wasted figures. The pictures on the walls were of the tumor under a microscope. Testicular cancer is a pathologist's nightmare. The neoplastic changes, rather than being confined to one kind of tissue—cancer of lung cells, cancer of brain cells—are a riotous orgy of the toti-potent tissue of would-be children, a microconglomerate of person: prostate, uterus, breast, lung, kidney, muscle, liver, all run together like an abstract painting. To a compulsive medical student like me, this violation of organized histology felt like seeing a bizarre and perverse monster. It was like turning over a rock in a smooth path of thought and seeing the crawling things of the unconscious. After my last patient, I drove home exhausted. Safe for a while because it was too late to call.

"How are the kids?" I kept my voice light.

"Terrific. No injuries, and Don got an A on his math test. You look terrible. Did the chairman call you in? No, that's not it. It's death. You have that look. Did one of your patients suicide?"

"We'll talk. At dinner."

When I stopped by the boys' bedrooms, they were sleeping peacefully. Ross, with unoperated adenoids, was on his back, noisy. Don, on his abdomen, was holding a pillow like a companion. I practiced saying good-bye, bathing in cheap melodrama: the organ music on record, a headstone shaped like a cut-down tree, hired mourners, and a black Ford hearse.

"I'm finished! Eighteen months of running subjects, and I'm through. If the factor analysis works, it won't be long now." Mary talked quickly as she watched me from behind her eyes. "I'll soon get rid of Pavlov and reinstitute William James in American psychology."

There were several minutes of silence as we ate salad. I didn't pick up her invitation for a round of academic banter about whether man was a gland, or was she right and man could decide.

"I have to talk to you about something. If I tell you then I'll hear it. Then I'll have to do something. Right now I'm paralyzed."

"What kind of trouble?" She stared unblinking.

"I have a small, very hard place on my left testicle."

"What does that mean?" She bit the corner of her lip.

"About twenty percent harmless cyst and eighty percent cancer. Three or four different kinds, and none of them is very nice."

White-faced, silent, she finally spoke, looking down at the table. "Is that the cancer the young physician patient of yours died of during your internship?"

"That's the one."

"You better get to the doctor quick. We'll throw everything at it. We'll do everything." She was grim.

"I'll do it tomorrow." Relieved that I would, now, but empty. My old world was already dying. Once death shows a person his alienation, the mourning for a lost world begins.

We both slept poorly, wandering the house as though alternating watches during a time of danger. I saw myself being lowered into the ground.

The next day I spent the early morning hours writing a paper. Since childhood my insulating dope was my work—thinking in a world apart, I could make it be any way I wanted. I called a little after nine.

"I have something potentially dangerous, maybe fatal. The doctor should look at it as soon as possible." The nurse told me it would be a five-week wait. Though tempted to use this escape, I poured it on. "I'm a psychiatrist on the faculty."

"Oh, I see." Her voice changed. Was it that I was a physician and therefore a dependable reporter, or a psychiatrist with distorted perceptions?

"He's tight, but I think I can make room around two. Get here at one forty-five so I can start a chart."

My restlessness was overwhelming. Mary was to meet me at the urologist's office. A walk on my ward and some discussion with patients made me wonder why we thought psychotics were unfortunate.

It was a waiting room full of old men who couldn't urinate. A young man in a urologist's office is venereal disease or testicular cancer. After a while my name was called.

Dr. Willard Goodwin, short, muscular, energetic, reminded me with laughter about our last workshop together on the subject of impotence. His ingenious advice was that the men take home pornography and masturbate slowly, making it last as long as possible. We argued in front of the class about why it worked. I said that it was he, as father, giving permission; he answered with practice makes perfect.

He was calm and efficient. "Take your pants down and let me take a look at it." He palpated carefully and then did a rectal examination. He felt deeply in my abdomen for lymph nodes. We went to his office to talk.

"We'll go to surgery first thing in the morning. We have to see it right away." He sat at one end of a couch, I on the other. A gleaming, ivory, four-foot penis bone of a whale was on the coffee table in front of us.

"How do you know it isn't a cyst? Maybe an old infection. Was my prostate soft? Why don't you put me on antibiotics for a few weeks and see?"

"Hey, let's stop playing games. You know we can't wait, and you know the numbers." He sat looking in my blue eyes with his blue eyes. I'd stare the bastard down.

"You fuckin' surgeons are all the same. You just gotta operate. Go to a food store and you get food. Go to a surgeon and he wants to cut. That's why I'm in another branch of medicine. To save people from the likes of you." My voice got louder as I got less sure.

"I want you in the hospital by six o'clock tonight for some blood tests. We'll go at seven in the morning. Nothing by mouth after four this afternoon."

"So that's the way it's going to be." I was talking to myself. Deflated but calmer. There was safety in his take-charge strength. Goodwin the Magnificent would lead, and I'd be a dumb body. We shook hands as I left. The back of my shirt was wet.

Mary and I walked around the campus. We planned quietly, without drama. Her parents would stay with the children, who would be told that it was a diagnostic procedure until we knew differently. She would get two children's books about death. One was about a bird, another about a grandmother who died at home. Mary's strained face was frozen, staring through things.

When we got home the kids were playing in the backyard with Mary's parents. I felt miles away. My wife, in-laws, and children would be the living unit until the new man arrived. Mary whispered with her parents. Don tried to keep squirming Ross from escaping a large packing box. I watched with distant curiosity. Sometimes my deadness was interrupted by a flash of fury. Why me? In anger I watched my neighbors work in their gardens, retrieve their newspapers, and call their dogs. Why not them? Why was it me who wasn't going to hear the third and fourth movements or find out what my boys' early traits were going to become? My father kept me indoors to practice when all the guys were playing outside; I watched them, face pressed to the window. Here I was again.

After my surgery, around the medical center I was a dead man. The scuttlebutt was that the sword hung by a frayed thread. My alienation was total. No one knew how to talk with me. Everyone struggled with his own feelings. No one was with me. I tried to flush them out with outrageous statements. They held onto their cover by agreeing. I brought up the topic and made gallows humor; they answered with sick grins. An occasional hero marched in, but so gruffly as to frighten. Living on another plane, a stranger, depressed and moody, I hid in my office. The pain of identification with me was more than anybody wanted. I was dead without the decency to crawl in the ground.

"Watch the endless parade of waves." We'd taken a postoperative trip from Los Angeles to the shores of La Jolla. Directing the final movement of a symphony, perhaps the *Eroica*, she was telling me how to stand. Death was to be a petty detail. My brain refused.

Thirty-one, with young children, a still-fresh career, my middle brain demanded survival. My talons wanted to hang on, yes, for dear life. In a desperate scramble for safety on ugly and slippery slime, I didn't want to slide into quiet submission. My middle brain, my red brain, wanted back into the karmic wheel, a world of sexuality, anger, and pain, the gritty feeling of work. To live in the endless activity of my laboratory, my patients and their troubles, my students and their demands. Lectures would give me the escape of the performing artist. I wanted the dirt of life under my fingernails. I refused to give in to death; I refused to flee.

They'll have to come get me. Rip me off my perch. Kill me. I'll fight until there isn't strength anymore. Alone, the last man, with my guns loaded, I was ready to go down fighting.

"Mary, I can't stay. We're on a La Jolla cliff looking down at the beauty of that beach, and it's a postcard. I feel teased. I hate it! I have to go back to work."

"I don't understand. You feel cheated out of life's beauty, and here it is and you don't want it."

"Don't you see? I'm not ready. My brain isn't ready. I don't even want to talk about it."

A furiously engaged brain doesn't have time for images of wasting bodies. There was no past spiritual work to make it another way. If I escaped from this tight place, I would spend time preparing myself for the next one. I promised. It takes a long time to prepare for death. If that work isn't done ahead of time, you leave with the middle brain's screams in your ears—fading in a falling, echoing reverberation.

SEVEN

I often wonder why it is that narcissism has become such an insulting word. A psychiatrist talking about a patient for whom his distaste has brimmed the container, even run down the side a little, is sure to use the word *narcissism* in his diagnostic report. The mechanical engineer, talking softly, shy in his one-room apartment, spending his weekends grinding the valves in his Porsche 911 and taking more night courses in computer programming, won't date girls after years of psychotherapy because he's narcissistic. The blond, breathless, dewy cosmetics executive whose orgasms go by so quickly with an ephemeral twitch—she's spent hours discussing the elusive event, wondering where the yawn went, with all her boyfriends, girlfriends, four psychiatrists, and an ob-gyn man who offered to circumcise her clitoris just like Marilyn Monroe's—is that way because she suffers from narcissism. The pop critic explained today's epidemic of TV situation comedies with the conclusion that people want to see only themselves. He predicts that the movement will culminate next season when for a small fee you can put video cameras all over the house and see yourself continuously with a commercial break every ten minutes. He called this trend narcissistic. In the world of psychiatry, if you want to stay home and play on your own piano, more than that, you want to play your own songs in your own way on your own piano, you may be considered to be narcissistic. Everybody is said to have too much, and I feel as though I didn't get enough.

As these things have had a wont to do, this once technical psychiatric word, *narcissism*, has leaked into general parlance. *The New York Review of Books* applied it to Paul Zweig when he drove his three-cycle car in the desert alone for a month instead of teaching English to minority students or taking his wife along; to Jerry Rubin when he switched from riling up the troops to taking sweat baths. I could add to the list all the leaders of the modern ecstatic religions including Chuck Dedrich, Claudio Naranjo, Alan Watts, Fritz Perls, Arthur Janov, Werner Erhard, all the women who don't want to have children, and my grandmother, who never stopped asking the question, if you don't take care of yourself, who in the world will? I think my father thought that if I learned to make myself feel good, not to need his smile so desperately, I'd escape.

When Freud was young and had a good disposition, *narcissism* had a different meaning than later in his life when he got so tired from trying to get patients out of themselves and into a therapeutic alliance. At a meeting of the Vienna Psycho-Analytic Society on November 10, 1909, he said that narcissism was a necessary step between autoeroticism and the love of others, but didn't specify just exactly where the energy was supposed to rest in this location that was halfway between your body and theirs. Maybe it was supposed to be like a transitional state in chemistry that no one sees either, sort of a high-potential energy plateau between two states of greater stability but lower energy—he had a way of borrowing imagery from more legitimate sciences, sometimes without even knowing it. It seems harmless to use *narcissism* that way, and if it helps theoreticians through a rough place, God knows they have enough ambiguity without us making them more trouble. But then the word got a little more malevolent.

In 1910, in his book on Leonardo (by then he was already beginning to wonder about the sexual source of the energy for such geniuses), Freud speculated about a reservoir of energy, free-floating, unattached to organs, and what we healthy people should do with it. In his most important paper on the subject, *On Narcissism, An Introduction* (1914), he began to make value judgments about where you should put your energy, just like my father did. Jung, by that time, had stolen a piece of free-floating energy and run away with it, calling it nonsexual libido. He later converted it into the electricity that lit up his system of temporal and spatial infinities, the universal unconscious. That was like when I wanted to go out and play instead of practicing my music. It made Freud plenty mad. If you had made up some energy, even though it seemed like plenty, and if you, like Freud, were laboring under the strict laws of thermodynamics, the compulsive bookkeeping of the science of his time, before quarks, a fellow worker just shouldn't run off with some of it. My father said that my not giving my all after his sacrifice was dishonest. There Freud was, after hours of listening to people talk about their vapors, doing the bookkeeping at night, and he discovered that some energy was missing. He went over the entry ledger, the records of flow, and the payout sheets and came up with a shortage. When he discovered who did it, he became angry with Jung and wrote a paper, *On Narcissism*, which I think was not only a way of claiming back the energy that Jung had stolen, but also began the tradition of analysts being irritated when they use the word *narcissism*.

As I understand it, the essence of the concept of narcissism is a resentment about some of a person's energy that he keeps to himself and won't use for your benefit. If you are a therapist and in charge of sharing energy with a person, you can begin to suffer from frustration. Narcissism, like pilfering at department stores, begins to mount up, and pretty soon your relationship is out of business. Also, psychiatrists, living peculiarly isolated lives, sitting alone listening to a shifting parade of others who spend the time talking about themselves, are unusually vulnerable to feelings of rejection, and if there's a way of turning that around into something that's the patient's fault, the concept of narcissism has real value. As my father used to say, how much of other people's selfishness should a person have to endure?

Narcissism, which could also be defined as a case of self-sufficiency of the brain, has social implications. I mean, if you're not dependent on people liking you to feel good, you can do what you want. If you have an un-poisoned supply of narcissism, the power of disapproving looks and the nightmares of being perceived in an un-attractive light would all be gone and then you could be, talk, act, feel, and dress as you wished. You could get intimate with yourself. If perchance you lost the connec-tions to your old sources of self-esteem, you wouldn't have to run around with your feeder hose in your hand, drip-ping, desperate to attach to another machine that would promise to smile. You could connect it to your own tank and feed yourself. You'd be free to leave. How often my heart must have wished I'd known how to do that.

Franz Alexander was the last of the three men who interviewed me for admission to the Southern California Psychoanalytic Institute. In those days one out of two psychiatrists who wished to receive this post-post graduate education was rejected. The criteria were vague: sensi-tivity, awareness of the irrational aspects of self, strength enough to cope with the sticky relationships that occur during psychoanalytic treatment. You couldn't be too well, or you wouldn't understand why some patients get nervous in the dark.

Alex, as he was known among his intimates, had for forty years been a free and mutinous theorist in the ever more rigidifying field of psychoanalysis. Freud's practice of political discipline—those who disagreed were put out of the tribe—had been taken up by the field's right-wingers. Left-wing Alex thought it was the therapeutic relationship rather than understanding the content of the unconscious that cured patients. His work was seen as

heretical pap and superficial by the psychoanalytic establishment. His free-ranging intellect had taken him beyond
psychoanalysis into such areas as the psychological influ-
ences on the thyroid gland. It was even said that, unlike
many analysts of his era, he thought the mind was in the
brain. I was eager to meet him as a hero and afraid about
what he might think of me. A close friend had recently,
been rejected for psychoanalytic training and he hadn't
learned why.

I was twenty-five years old when I saw him at the
Mount Sinai Medical Center in Los Angeles, where some
said at seventy he came to retire, and others that he had
sought political asylum from his enemies at the Chicago
Psychoanalytic Institute. I sat nervously in his waiting
room. The deeply tanned, white-haired, cherubic, ele-
gantly dressed short man looked through his thick glasses
at me from his open office door and beckoned me in. I
followed as he walked slowly, bent over, appearing un-
sure. I turned down my expectations—with a lifelong
love for fine cigars, too much food, and wine, his day was
obviously over. What of his newest papers? They sounded
so fresh. His slow and aimless shuffling of papers on his
desk alarmed me—suppose this senile old man wrote a
bad report? I sat in front of his desk, waiting, anxiously
sorting through game plans.

"So, Mandell, two ls, you come to the institute. Why?"
He clipped and lit a Dunhill, cleaned his glasses, and
peered nearsightedly over them for several moments before asking the question.

I had rehearsed this part. "I want to find out about
myself, and my goal of being a professor of psychiatry requires breadth in training, of outlook. Psychoanalysis is
one of the most important aspects of psychiatry." He
picked up a thin, black, German fountain pen, turned
back the cover on a tablet, and began making notes. My
hands were cold. I felt as if I was a worthwhile candidate,
but God knows what this shell of an erstwhile genius was
going to put down on that yellow paper.

"Just one? Wouldn't you say it is the core of psychiatry? The fundamental matrix of all psychiatry?" He watched my face with such a bland and unfocused expression that I thought he was establishing broad facts like species rather than particulars like feelings.

"Well, I . . ." Dare I take the chance? I used to think rebels liked other rebels. They don't. In fact, those who make a living out of rebellion feel usurped by other rebels. He didn't say anything, waiting, pen poised. My back began to sweat in his air-conditioned office.

I took a deep breath and said it fast. "To be honest, I think that psychoanalysis is really just one part of something far more important. . . . Psychoanalysis is the beginning of the new era of human brain biology."

"Of what?!" He put his pen down and folded his hands on the desk. His gaze got more focused.

"I have a feeling . . . well, a belief that the psychiatry of the future will involve the manipulation of brain chemistry, using things like exercise and drugs, and psychoanalytical observation will measure their effects . . . rather than assuming that the psychoanalytic process changes anything . . . the quality of the relationship, memories, dreams, fantasies will all be data from the brain used to measure its biological status . . . which will be organized into another theory . . . one that hasn't been written yet." His eyebrows were up. The hell with it, he probably wouldn't remember any of this anyway. ". . . no one thinks that the rash causes measles . . . a fantasy, a wish, a myth will be like the rash. Today we think they're like the virus. Ever since . . ."

"Where did you get such ideas?" His voice suddenly strong.

"Among other places, in your writings. Sandor Rado too. And Sherrington, Jackson, and from my own head— late at night in the cat lab."

"What about Freud? Did he write about such ideas?" Chin in hand and staring, he looked alert.

"If I told you when I really began to think like

this . . . I mean, it's really all about Freud. But I don't think I'm in a position to talk about it now . . . until my training gets a little further along . . . I have no right . . . see, I don't know about this except what I've read and . . ."

"Go on! Stop your obsequious drivel. Say what you're thinking!" His eyes didn't leave my face. I was excited by his attention, afraid about what it might mean.

"It's from Freud's *Project for a Scientific Psychology* . . . the letters he wrote Fliess. It became the core of the seventh chapter of his *Interpretation of Dreams* . . . which became the theory of psychoanalysis. I read it early in medical school. Then I realized where it came from . . . but, still, it's speculative, and I . . ."

"Yes, yes . . . go on."

"Freud had just returned from a visit with Fliess and he was up day and night writing for about three weeks . . . no sleep, no food, writing and rewriting. It was either a manic attack after the intimacy and the relief of being understood at last, or cocaine. Yes, cocaine. I think that Freud took cocaine to work from about eighteen eighty-three to eighteen eighty-five, maybe as late as eighteen ninety-three. The theory of instinctual excitation and its management . . . the whole story came from what cocaine does to the brain. Psychoanalytic theory is itself an example of what I think psychoanalysis will be used for in the future. The theory itself reflects the effects of a change in brain chemistry." I was on the edge of the chair, pointing, talking loudly, teaching. "His theories assume a constant source of instinctual excitement, sexual and aggressive urges demanding discharge, requiring the development of psychic structures like ego and superego and their functions to contain the excitement . . . symptoms come from the leakage of the excitement into other areas of psychological function. His diagrams of neurons supposed an everlasting, continuously regenerated supply of psychic excitement, energy, that needed a counterforce to control . . . making all things conflict . . . making efforts to deal with the excitement our defenses and resistances . . .

as though our selves came from the solidification of our fortress against the raging storms of our cocainized middle brains . . . the human psyche derived from corraling wild horses trying to kick out the slats of the fence. . . ." I paused for breath. Only one of his eyebrows had come down. I could hardly stop talking.

"Young man, Mandell with two ls, are you trying to tell me that psychoanalytic theory is a reflection of the chemistry of Freud's brain as it was changed by cocaine?"

"Well, something like that. What I think is that Freud described a cocaine slice of the brain. A psychology for the Darwinian survival brain. Cocaine emphasizes one orientation of the brain, like war, it's a good time to look at fear and aggression. He presented a cocaine view of the brain." I waited. Had I gone too far? He relit his cigar, leaned back in his chair, and stared at a corner of the ceiling for several minutes.

"So next you're going to say that Christ, during the seventeen unaccounted-for years, was in India not getting revelations or learning yoga but eating hallucinogenic plants? Early Christian spiritual philosophy reflects the hallucinogenic drug slice of the human brain?" He smiled for the first time when I nodded. He was amused.

"All right, Mandell, we have Freud and Christ diagnosed. How about you? What kind of example of brain function are you?"

"Well, I don't think I have too many problems."

"Name some." The pen was up again. I told him about my fears in medical school, the nail-biting, my intense competitiveness, my fear and rage with my father, my lower abdominal cramps, my allergies, my insomnia, and my occasional states of strange thoughts and intense imagery. My life in another world. He didn't seem to be listening. He was drawing concentric circles on his yellow pad.

"Your dreams. What are they like?"

"I have three types. One is that I didn't study for an exam or didn't even know I was taking a course until the day of the test. Panic, struggle, fear of failure. I wake up sweating. Another recurrent one is a' wax museum. It's got some of the strange quality that I told you invades my waking thoughts. My fantasies get frozen and I walk among them. The men in my life. The ones I both hate and want to be like. A third type I have once in a while is in a carnival . . . tawdry, loud music, bizarre; happy faces get twisted. I get frightened and . . ."

"How do you eat?" I was confused by the interruption.

"Well, ever since I was a child I've struggled with my weight. My mother was always rushing to the table with plates of food, trying to put out the fires of my father's temper . . . so food is a treatment for nervousness. . . . Also I love good food and . . ."

"No. I mean, *when* do you eat?"

"I have no breakfast but coffee and . . ."

"You have no appetite in the morning?"

"I don't feel like eating until early evening."

"Then what?"

"Well, I have a light dinner and then . . ."

"You get a ravenous appetite late at night?"

"Exactly. If I'm not careful, I'll clean out the refrigerator."

"All night? Open the refrigerator, close the refrigerator, work, and back to the refrigerator?"

"Exactly. Since I was twelve or thirteen. It gets worse when I'm tense."

"For sweets? How much of your favorite ice cream can you eat in one night?" He was jotting as we talked. I had lost a sense of where he was going.

"Sometimes more than a gallon. Once one of those things gets started, I can't stop it. What do you make . . . what does it mean?" I was growing uncomfortable.

"It's a classical case of sporadic bulimia. A buried psychosis of the body. It goes with your excitability, your strange thoughts. You've buried your insanity under intellectual theories and body symptoms; the latent psy-

chosis that goes with allergies, abdominal pain . . ." He
started to write vigorously on the yellow pad.

"Wait! Wait! Don't put that down. For God's sake!
Sporadic bulimia. That's what psychotics have who eat
so much they rupture their esophagus. Buried psychosis!
You can't put that down. The institute . . . they couldn't
possibly . . . wait a minute." I was beside myself. I just
knew this was going to happen. That senile old man!
There was a long silence.

"So, you're not ready to be a rebel yet, Mandell with
two ls. Not a real one. You young men with new thoughts
think you're separating yourselves from the fathers with
all that wild talk—some of it even makes sense. But it's
not really new, because it's not free. You have to be detached from, not hating, what was. Hate and rebellion
stick you right to the thing you're trying to get away from.
Wanting to kill your father makes you as dependent on
him as needing his food and protection. Dealing with this
problem is what your psychoanalysis is going to be about.
How would you say it? You're going to have to deal with
the father slice of your brain!"

My education was shopping for pieces of people. I
would outfit myself with a combination of the people I
admired. Humanistic but tough, idealistic but practical,
creative yet persevering. Models were hard to find.

"Gene, I don't exactly know how to say this, but I
think I've chosen the wrong specialty." I was near tears
and talking to Eugene Pumpian-Mindlin, my psychotherapy guru at UCLA's Neuropsychiatric Institute. A
scholar in the European tradition, his depth, kindness, and
wisdom made him beloved by us students—those of us
frightened by patients who had problems in the complex
sphere of the brain. Short, balding, and baggy, he wore
an omnipresent pipe and a pair of sandals. He had the
sensitivity of one who had been sick and experienced loss.
He owned a perspective that prevented the necessary degree of male madness to grind out Brownie-point papers

for the cold committees of the academy. Later, students would riot to protect such professors.

"Sit down and tell me about it." He pointed to the safe, big, soft, brown leather chair by his desk. He lit his pipe.

"You know that patient I've been telling you about, the pretty one with the impulse disorder?" My voice was shaking. "I don't think I better see her anymore. And I think I have to get out of psychiatry."

"Why's that?" The rhythm of his puffing didn't change.

"Because of her goddamn legs. I can't think of anything else. She's in there talking about her college grades and all I can think about are her legs. Her skirts are getting shorter and her neckline lower. She's got me. I'm going into internal medicine or neurology. I feel terrible all the time. Last night I couldn't sleep. A doctor who's going to be a psychiatrist can't be like that! Don't remind me about the stuff about an aggressive use of sexuality and Fenichel's concept of a vagina with teeth. I thought all about that, and it didn't do any good."

Sweet Gene. How did he know that guilt rather than a sexual urge was driving my compulsive thoughts? After puffing on his pipe for a while, it seemed to me for hours, he said, "Well, Arnold, you know you can fuck your patients—just don't call it psychotherapy."

I was stunned. I snuck a look at him and caught a twinkle in his eyes. I understood. Laughter started and wouldn't stop. Tears ran, the relief was so enormous. That afternoon my patient had a therapist. We explored her feelings of worthlessness; sleeping promiscuously with men gave her a feeling of being wanted. Several weeks later she got to the part about using sex to "reduce men to size."

How to escape from a system that worships power, cruel power, over all other human values? The symbolic act of riddance, grand and dramatic, was publishing a book about my experience in professional football which told the truth. God! Was there anger over *The Nightmare Season*! The mean male father voices got so loud, so threatening, so furious, so amazed at my audacity. In vengeance the owner of the San Diego Chargers went to the reporters and fumed dramatic distortions about my drug research, making me Doctor Dope in the newspapers as far away as Jakarta. Once I heard a bearded guru say, while looking down from his perch practicing T'ai Chi yoga on a high wooded knoll over dirty, bay beach water in downtown San Francisco, "Sometimes you have to blow yourself out."

"Doc, what were you giving all that mescaline to chickens for?" The narcotics officer walked right into my laboratory office without calling first, flashed his identification card, and sat down. It was eight months after the football noise started, and by then my drug safe had been examined by the inspectors twice; my car had been stopped once as they looked for drugs in the glove compartment because a car like mine had been reported to be involved in drug smuggling from Mexico; I heard clicking on my phone even after I stopped my answering service; and a member of the government drug establishment had reviewed my prescriptions with me, asking for justifications. I was becoming convinced that the new janitor who cleaned up my lab at night was an undercover narc.

"How did you find out that we gave mescaline to chickens?" He showed me a xeroxed copy of one of our recent papers. "Who sent it to you?" There's a sudden suffusion of warmth of the body that goes along with paranoid fear.

"It just arrived one day in the mail, and I checked with our computer and found out that you don't have a Schedule I permit for research with mescaline, so I came here to find out under whose permit you'd been doing the work."

I couldn't imagine who would be so angry with me as to send the local narcotics officer a copy of some work we did on the process of habituation in chickens. He was smirking as though he were waiting for me to confess that I was really not giving the drug to chickens but that my two thousand square feet of laboratories, seven technicians, two Ph.D. candidates, four postdocs, and several undergraduate and medical students were just a cover for selling mescaline for five dollars a jolt to hippies. He wore a bright checked sport coat of nonshrinking shine and unmatching checked pants. Two kinds of Kandinski graph paper pasted together. His pink bow tie matched his face, his under-the-chin fat was ridged by a tight collar, and he wore shiny brown bluchers over red-checked socks. He looked about thirty-five and not entirely unpleasant.

"Listen, Doc, I know you're doing important work. I read all about it in *People* magazine. I wouldn't want to bother you for no reason, but the regs say that for you to do research with Schedule I drugs you have to have a permit. Also I have to put down here," he was carrying a clipboard with a white pad attached, "what your research with mescaline and chickens is about."

We had gotten into mescaline work only briefly so hadn't applied for a permit. It takes so many months to get one, and we had a new idea to try. "We were using Shulgett Rantzoff's permit. He's got one for mescaline in Berkeley, and this is animal, not human work." I felt nervous. My stomach was rolling and I could feel the moistness begin under my arms, the cold feeling in my fingers. It had been this way for eight months. Being made to feel like a dope dealer, a criminal, a freaky bad guy.

"Doc, you know that the permit is for the drug, the investigator, and the geographical location too. I mean, you can't use Rantzoff's permit . . ."

"But we work in collaboration. You see his name on that paper there, along with mine and Fritz Krisp."

"Krisp? That name sounds familiar. Was he involved in the football thing too?"

There it was. The feds don't pay attention in the gray areas until the media stick them up in the air, and then they worry them like scratching a rash. Each agency has to have its own report on them in case a reporter comes. Or a distant supervisor makes an inquiry. The feds may even like you, but they have to make a report and the legislation is so murky that you can't be perfect and that's why they don't come around until the threat of the media makes them.

I never know how to deal with law-enforcement people. Whether it's my getting a ticket for driving slow in the fast lane or these guys coming into my laboratory, I react neurotically with fear and start to run my speeded, high-flown pitch, and they look confused. But I think it's disapproval and so I try harder. I move from neurobiology to astrophysics, from Boolean algebra to Whitehead, from quotes from Gautama on the futility of asceticism to the Four Noble Truths, and pretty soon their confusion turns to irritability. Then I imagine that they see through my intellectual defenses, these primitive but shrewd seekers of the truth, these taxi drivers with high purpose, and I confess everything. That I think chemicals will soon rule the mind of man, that I am a witch with a mania for power, making extracts from the fruit of strange bushes, and soon sending a specially nourished pigeon to take a crap in the tea of the President of the United States when he's in the Rose Garden of the White House and we'll control the world. My only hope is that as Raskolnikov works desperately at clarifying his motive for the crime, the officer, in his humanity, unfreezes and takes me home to dinner.

"OK. We'll take care of the permit business later. Why don't you just tell me what you've been doing with the chickens?" He pulled himself up into a neat, tidy position, clipboard on his lap, Scripto ball-point in hand. He looked as eager as those in the front row of my classes, early in the series of lectures when it seems as though it's going to be a series of stand-up comedy acts for which they're going to get credit—before they find out the stuff is difficult.

"We've worked for several years on the problem:

why do we stop noticing things? I mean, we come into a new room and notice things, and then we come into the room again a little later and we probably are used to the first things we've seen and don't see them anymore, but see some other things, and then we come into the room again and we've seen it all, so the next time we go into the room we don't see anything. We sit down on the couch and read a newspaper or call somebody on the phone." I was waving my arms, indicating the coming in and going out of the room with my right hand; my left hand was the room.

"So you've got the chickens in houses?" He had drawn a box on his pad of paper and began to put several small xs in it.

"No, not exactly. See, first I'm trying to explain the underlying principle, the thing we're trying to get at. Then I'll be more precise." He relaxed against the back of the couch. My office wall is full of certificates. Thirty-seven of them. I often let my eyes wander the walls to fortify me. I stopped at a research prize I had won in 1962 for finding an unusual compound in the body fluid of schizophrenics. I never found out what it was, even after years of trying to extract and identify it. I think the award was given to me for boiling all that urine.

"The psychologists working in the area call the process *habituation*. If you were sitting in this office and I had a lie detector apparatus strapped to you . . ."

"They don't let us use those things anymore, though if it weren't for that I would have never caught those Chicano . . ."

"No. I don't mean we'd use the lie detector setup for catching somebody. I would put it on you for research."

"Wouldn't you need my permission?"

"Let's go at this another way. Suppose, with his permission, I'm doing a research project on a man in a room and you are watching. Now just imagine . . ." He closed his eyes. "Imagine that the subject of the experiment is connected to a polygraph and I drop a pail full of bells.

He'd jump. The polygraph would register a blip signifying a response of his autonomic nervous system, his sweat glands, his blood vessels. He would be startled."

"A pailful of bells!" He opened his eyes and looked at me with what could pass for the beginnings of reverence.

"If I kept dropping the pail, regularly, rhythmically, pretty soon his polygraphic indicators would stop registering. His brain would have habituated, that's what we call it. He would stop responding to the stimulation." He was nodding his head now. Eyes open, he was writing. A number of small bells were appearing in the box along with the xs. He inked in the bells so they were solid.

"The process by which subjects stop responding to repeated sensory stimulation we call habituation, and we're studying the chemistry . . . ."

"Doc, I don't know how to tell you this, but if you were dropping a pailful of bells every so often, I just wouldn't stop paying attention. First off, it's loud, right? Second, it's a real strange thing to do. See, in my field, we're taught to pay particular attention to anyone doing unusual things. Even though it may not look like it's illegal. See, we've found, I mean I'll never forget the lecture on the subject because they told us about a lot of weird stuff that they first picked up on that later turned out to be the key to finding a real criminal act. You've seen it on television, they call them suspicious characters." I was close to the tears of impotence and to intense motivation at the same time. I couldn't run the hundred-yard dash very fast and this kid used to ride me about my slowness and I would get these tears while racing that would make it very difficult for me to see.

"Have you ever been in a topless bar?" I looked straight into his eyes—as I would after waiting three years, three times a week, before asking a woman patient directly about all the innuendos she'd been making about her father's sexual activities with her.

He blushed, looked down, and giggled. "Can't say I haven't."

"OK! Now tell me, how long did it take you to stop looking at the tits and get into conversation with your buddies so that it could have been any old bar?"

"Hey, Doc. You've got something there! You really do. Shit, I used to complain that after paying double for drinks, how come it don't make any difference after a while?" I felt the muscles in my thighs relax.

"That process of not caring any more about something that got your attention in the first place, we call habituation."

"How do you spell that, Doc? I want to get it right." I spelled it and watched him carefully print it on top of the box with the xs and bells in it.

"Mescaline is a tool for examining the chemistry of that process. We think that we can prevent habituation; we can keep both the familiarity of old knowledge and the feeling of newness. The combination of old mastery and the feeling of discovery is, we think, the essence of creativity."

"Doc, are you telling me that if a person took mescaline he would continue to get horny over those tits?" I nodded. He shook his head in wonderment. "I guess that's what they meant in that *People* magazine article when they said you guys were pushing back the old barriers of science. Wow!" He put a big circle around the box and then traced around it several times so that it began to look as though it were receding down a tunnel.

"Look, Doc, I know you're busy. I'll just tell them that your chicken work has to do with seeing. Helping people to see better. It seems to me that nobody can get mad if you're trying to help the blind. It sure *is* a kind of blindness." He got up, shook my hand, his as wet as mine was cold, and left the office.

EIGHT

Going to die can't be handled by redefinition. Call it an intellectual defense or fear of raw experience, I usually bite off a small piece of perception and race back to my head cave, wash it, examine it, take it apart, reassemble it in various ways, and then glue it together, making something of my own. Grass becomes cud and I lecture on the fundamental mushiness of lawns. In the face of death, my brainwork, instead of bringing me comfort, increased the feelings of entrapment. In 1965 I realized that, entombed all my life in my head, I would now be buried in earth. Where was the light, the life, the beauty to which all this climbing work, pleasure put-off, was supposed to lead? My soul wanted out. Screamed for a release from rationality, from the boxes of my brain. I wanted the civilized chess game my marriage had become to turn into an orgy for women and animals, bombing the library, and doing a nasty on the White House lawn. The feeling got stronger. There was no escape inside; only the outside was left.

The glimpse of life I saw when I woke from the opiate fog and amnesia of my cancer surgeries was the bluebells. Among the empathic flowers, guilty flowers, thank-God-it's-not-me flowers, administratively indicated flowers, owed flowers, early funereal flowers, was this bunch of wild flowers with no tag. Mary, trying, soft-spoken

103

crazy, asked the florist who had sent them; the answer was that the sender wished to remain anonymous. Strung taut in the threatened dissolve of her world, a child not yet ready to be on her own, a life-mate wife with the fear of the pain of tearing commingled roots, she became suspicious and angry, looking for an enemy in place of the death she couldn't find. She fussed about my visits from demanding research assistants (your family comes first at a time like this) ; my parents (no offer of monetary assistance; no comfort in your mother's talk; your father refuses even to visit) ; and the anonymous flowers. I didn't know who sent them, but they lightened what had become all death and blame.

The bunch said pretty and wild. Wild flowers. Wild. That was the feeling, the only feeling, that promised escape—from the dead wood of the bench on which I sat waiting to see if the marbles of cancer had arrived in my chest X ray, my eyes making Orthodox Jewish wooden burial boxes from the acoustic tiles on the ceiling. Lying in bed, skinny with the starvation of depression, the trustful connection with Mary broken, raging at the Fates, seeing the worried puzzlement in my sons' faces at my weakened condition, I searched my brain for an escape. A place that didn't bleed, that didn't ache, that wasn't the end. There was only one. Wild.

Carole was then, as now, a professor of psychiatric nursing. Ten years, between then and now, have given her a rich husband, two sons, a Mercedes convertible, but I wonder if they sated her hunger. That hunger of hers, an affirmation of life, that I lived on for eight months of escape ten years ago. The tender bath, those flowers again, bring it all back. Ten years ago she was a twenty-five-year-old new professor. I lectured to her nursing class. We talked a few times. I gave her a book. Then cancer came and she sent the flowers that weren't signed.

I got home after ten friction-filled, TV-tragic days in the hospital to sympathetic looks. Mary's folks, afraid and kind, were there with the commitment and grim flatness of northern Anglo-Saxons under siege. The boys, frightened, were quiet in their routines. Mary, unable to sleep, or to be awake, not quite finished in her Ph.D.ing, running quickly out of lifetime security with each potential metastasis (the security of filled bed, cupboard, and brain space), began a panicked dash to her degree. In an emotionally dead house, I changed seats in the living room often, shuffling bent over in the pain of whole-body hemisection, starving at 122 pounds, visited as a sad-faced ex-person by a few friends, empty, dead, hopeless. Against the depressed bitterness of my brain, the same slabs of cooked meat and bland salads, the dinners of thirteen years of marriage, unnoticed when served with the gravy of her beauty, brilliance, and vivacity, became a message of uncaring. Childish, sullen, silent, I couldn't eat. The house, in the book piles and dishevelment of stunted genius students forever, became an intolerable final resting place. The immobilization of my depression prevented escape to the brightly colored test tubes of my laboratory. Where could I go? I was a traitor for wanting to.

One day she called. Carole was so labored in her casualness that I guessed the source of the wild flowers. The conversation was brief, but it seeded fantasies that brought a rising vitality that started in the legs and straightened my bentness. Suddenly, there was life. After her call, I made two pieces of cinnamon toast and a glass of milk—they tasted good. I imagined what this otherwise cool, blond Scandinavian would do with a Russian para-Mediterranean at her controls. I might discover that a Trojan horse with a gypsy in its hindquarters had been allowed into the right and proper nursing faculty. The images brought an energy, a hope.

Shortly after her call, I got another. Shielded for weeks from the calls of my patients, I got this one because he was locked in his bedroom with an army pistol and said that he was going to put it in his mouth. A mathematician, a computer specialist, he was not one for histrionics. I left the house for the first time, almost welcomed the cut-in-half pain of operating the clutch of my car's manual transmission, climbed the stairs to his room, and three hours later got the gun. I thanked him. He smiled when he realized he had rescued his psychiatrist.

I couldn't go back to my peopled, empty house. Two blocks away from home the blue wild flowers moved in the breeze. I drove to the school, found her address, and arrived at her door with my chest pounding. She wore a light summer dress and met me without surprise. Bright colors, wine rack, antique table, scatter rugs, and a black furry bedspread. She showed me a large stuffed lion she made while waiting. There were no words. I sat on the couch and grabbed her with the hunger of the starved. I went first to her mouth, then her neck, through her blouse, to her navel. We rolled and chased and got naked.

God how we ran. Night races in my new, used red Porsche along Sunset Boulevard, with drunk teenagers who drove Corvettes and gave me the finger. Playing jazz piano all night in black bars, drinking straight rum and with a blonde on my arm. Polaroid pictures taken using mirrors. Fucking in a phone booth near the Troubador on little Santa Monica. In the shrill scream of last-minute living, I was unreachable. I was too busy to take dying Mary to a movie.

In eight months the flight for life was over. The stuck-to-the-floor accelerating brain gland of mine changed from bright red, through a shaky orange, to yellow, to black. I told all, asked for my beating, sold my Porsche, and never saw Carole again. It got very bad at my house. Hours of cross-examination, sorting through every inch of the entrails of the corpse, night-wakening talking panics, the frightened rage of a twice-left woman. I waited every three months to walk the last mile for my chest X ray, baby-sat, cooked, apologized endlessly, and sat in a darkened university office, too destroyed to do anything. Carole stopped calling, lost twenty pounds, recovered, and got married. Mary and I were dead. It was never the same. The movie marriages of our adolescent years were to last forever. The glamorously endowed princess, with the un-spoken sensual need, sat primly as the suitors lined up. When one was chosen and the others beheaded, it was a privilege that must be honored.

Can playmates live together beyond the fracture of their playhouse? When you spend as much time together, intimate young time, as we had—then you are each other. I cry for me and her. She does the same. It took ten years of careful disengagement, and quiet, excruciating pain, but it's finally so that each of us is free to move on, if we can.

Now, ten years later, the flowers are back, but this time I know an answer isn't in the drunken convulsions of the middle brain, the temporary amnesia from the shock treatment of orgasm, a manic flight. But where? A path going higher, an escape into the upper brain, away from the dangerous precipice that threatens with a fall into intimacy and caring, attachment, and pain? Shall I take a Jesuit's high flight into celibacy, the cold steely edge, impenetrable, of good works, rewarded by prideful exhaustion and emotional safety? Fearful, I practice starv-ing my needs. I've learned that forever-echoing vibrations of karma are created by small movements of the middle brain for territorial linebackers like me. Pleasure isn't easy. Food, that forkful of Mother, brings coronaries. Wild flowers, chaos.

In anxious defense, my brain has twisted the women of my head into caricatures.

Baby Doll, with small pink labia, pubis shaved, swathed in black sheer underwear, requires dependent care. We become so intrigued with her body, the sensuality of her descriptions of its little messages, that the medicine chest becomes full of drugs, the afterconversation about constipation. I'm busy looking down her throat, feeling her forehead, writing a prescription, and playing doctor in the bushes between two garages. I separate and massage her behind in a hurry before our mothers catch us.

With Literary Lady I sit over ouzo on ice and contrast the female prose of Katherine Anne Porter with the phallic words of Henry Miller. A linear arrangement of pencils is on her desk, the books on the shelves are according to subject, the douche bag hangs over the shower nozzle. An everlasting undergraduate, she has eroticized term papers into episodes of sadomasochism with her professors. I hear several times her story of being masturbated by her drunken father and we read Oedipal themes into the tales of the homosexual playwrights. The raptures of rhetoric are her most fulfilling contractions.

I lie under this hospital blanket and feel a penis that is soft with fear, shriveled with disuse. I trace one scar from the empty testicular sac on the left to the navel; another crosses the first and goes around my left side to my spine. Touching the scars feels funny. Peculiar and unexpected twinges, an alien spread of electricity where Mary's hand made soft and safe touches. It's like me and my penis trying to function in a new place. I think about it, but the doors to the feeling are closed.

There's another problem for me. Something has changed in women of late. The power part of sex has shifted. It seems as though it's the women who move, choose, evaluate, and decide. Already prone to feeling that my performance is being criticized in all things, from piano improvisation to parallel parking, I find myself on nervous trial. A loose metal disc is anchored to the coronal ridge of my tap-dancing penis. I hear the rhythmic whisper of brushes on a snare drum as I hop up and down trying to impress with one-legged time steps. ". . . oh, hambone (shuffle, shuffle, shuffle), dance you hambone . . . oh, hambone (shuffle, shuffle, shuffle), dance, you hambone . . ."

I worry about the emotional price. Taught by ceaseless, painful, and cathartic lectures from a tortured mother ("If you ever make a woman feel like your father makes me feel, I'll haunt you . . . I'll come back from the dead if necessary"), I feel I owe a lot more than any hooker dare charge. The taciturn toughies of my movie era talked mean and gentled their ladies into featherbeds, slapping only in cases of uncontrollable hysteria and foreplay. Our generation was trained to care. Cradled in the safety of my muscular and everlasting security, my woman's legs could spread, her vagina run like the side of a sweating mountain, her ecstasy could break loose, and riding with her would sweep me around bends and over falls with uncontrollable rushes. I watch for Indians, make sure of the food supply, and buy another insurance policy.

The liberated new ladies don't understand my fear. "I'm telling you it's always the same with you guys. Afraid of the involvement, the obligation, the burden. So who gave it to you? We have a wonderful weekend and then you bring up an unexpected business trip. It's always the same: 'I haven't recovered from my bad experiences; my analyst tells me it's a basic problem I have with intimacy, so don't take it personally.' Do you know what? I'm dating shvartzers now because at least they don't pretend to be anything but honeybees. What the hell is becoming of you men? Can't you just be?"

It's a piece of work left for my second cycle.

NINE

"Ron, I've done what I could: every kind of psychiatric thinking, self-examination, hours of meditation. I'm telling you, the helper can't be helped. The meaning is gone, Ron, do you understand? All my life I've lived on it, and now I can't find any."

"Arn, it's a depression. You know they're time-limited. It'll go away and then things will look different. How many cases have we seen together? You've got to have . . ."

"I have an idea. One idea. It's been haunting me. I know you won't see it my way. You'll think it's psychotic. It's about a path from death in the first cycle into a fresh second cycle. Out of a blackened middle brain into the blue-white of the upper one. High and free."

"I never understand what you're talking about with this red- and white-brain business. What is it in real words? Have we talked about it?"

"No. And I'm not ready. I have to think about it some more."

"But you can tell *me*."

"Not even you. Not yet."

"Is it one of your new biochemical ideas?"

"No, and don't ask."

"OK, Arn. Just promise me you won't do anything

impulsive. I mean, you'll talk to me before you do anything?"

"If I can."

It has always been easier to speculate about who is a
good psychotherapist than about what's good in psychotherapy. The medical mind being what it is, the activities
of psychotherapists are described as procedures. They are
really persons.

I know of a world-record long-distance runner whose
leg was burn-withered in infancy, a touring golf professional with an atrophied arm from childhood polio. The
best social scientists I know are so naive about the conduct
of their interpersonal affairs as to tax one's credulity. Natural psychotherapists live in psychic pain around a crack
that opens into their insanity. They have alienated shyness
and a depressive's hunger for contact, raw nerve endings
and enough strength to stand their feelings. Only the
manufactured therapists carry out procedures.

For the first several years of my professional life I
knew what I was doing: supplying, if not agreement, the
feeling of being understood; finding ways to like people
whom few others did; helping to clarify jumbled thoughts;
using dreams and memories to help the patient bring
murky and distorted events of the past under the consid-
eration of his adult intelligence; examining our relationship as evidence of what the patient does with the significant people in his life; cheerleading and sometimes cuffing
the now-attached patient into an independent life. I
learned it. I did it. I taught it. I believed it. The tripartite
apparatus of id, ego, and superego was its anatomy. Survival instincts, twisted in expression, energized the dis-
eases. I pushed and pulled, nodded and waited, grabbed
things speeding by, for display to the patient, endured the
displaced rages with the ghost of Freud patting me on the
back for my grit, and hoped that I was doing some good.
The highest price was in the surrender of my fantasy
life—to be honestly earning the hourly fee, you must live

in the life of your patient. They come to stay in your head, talking again while you drive or are in the shower. Saying understanding uh-huhs while having your own daydreams is stealing. Playing golf in that dark room is malpractice. In silence, through thousands of measures of string and woodwind chitchat, I wait to strike a gong. At day's end, the muscles around my shoulders ache like those of a rock crusher, a peculiar twist, since the patient wields the hammer.

As I approached thirty-five the fervor started to burn out and I began not to understand. A patient came to me who was hopelessly sick. I was the last in a line of psychiatrists; a two-year hospitalization was planned. After fifteen years of rocking in and out of doorways before entering, washing his hands until they bled, and snapping his fingers continually when outside his house, the man got completely well (for four years that I know of) after the second session when I asked him directly about his masturbatory fantasies. On the other hand, a mildly nervous housewife, three children and husband well cared for, active, bright, energetic, melted and grew languorously adhering within three months, drowned in primitive sexual fantasies and the hallucinated voices of the men in her phone. It took three years of difficult and dangerous work to get back to where we started. The experts explain how all this happens with the mumbo jumbo of a catechism—internally consistent but out in left field.

Things became dada. Psychotherapy was the lifesaving argument of two immigrants who were on a boat that sank coming to America; gesticulating wildly kept them afloat while the waves swept them to shore. Psychotherapy was what a skinny, ugly call girl who earned three hundred a night taught me about the factors in her success: *griv* sense (the capacity to intuit the interpersonal and sexual style desired without being told—dominance, submission, activity, passivity) and never have an orgasm with a client (conducting the interaction properly distanced). Psychotherapy was the hairdresser who sells his client a new self that she can see in the mirror—the hypnosis lasting until the next comb-out. Psychotherapy was what the neighborhood bars and their tenders offer in a combination of chemotherapy and group process. What are we doing for our money, we, the full-time psychotherapists who don't give our patients an orgasm, hairdo, or drinks?

Do we create *more* trouble? The new breed of community psychiatrists have taken all the human dignity from the flophouse, the town greeter waving on the street corner, the village drunk, guttersnipe, bench polisher, and nut. We've swept away these valuable social institutions and in their place put diagnoses, a courtroom for commitment, the hospital ward, and an ever-more-bizarre group of psychotherapies.

Pychotherapy, like all art movements in their last days, has become degenerate. Or is it my problem with lost meaning? What was once a group of techniques for changing man's conscious experience has become a new set of shoulds, group invasions of the private soul, righteous ritual, personal charisma, fad, the rigidity of institutions, and the growing desperation of customers who were promised too much. The language and vision have invaded all of life: from a French physician recommending a gentle delivery to avoid birth trauma (what?!) to the garbled psychoanalysis of a *New York Times* book review (". . . while avoiding the language, she has described beautifully the shock and emptiness of the discovery of her absent penis and her anger at her brother who . . .").

It sounds like a zoo. The hungry noises of a frenetic search for the release from bondage that will accompany the second coming of something, anything. The roars begin after smelling the newest meat in *Psychology Today*: primal screams; sensual groans of naked Esalen mud bathers; quiet chants of practitioners of Theravada, Mahayana, Tantra, and Zen; grunts from a forceful Rolfing; macho curses of a Synanon game; black marching boots moving to the rhythm of est; the righteous lecture of a strict vegetarian; the unhooked uh-huhs of today's burned-out psychoanalyst; bitter, funny stories of Alcoholics Anonymous; screams of triumph and despair during the weighing rituals of Take Off Pounds Sensibly; the bebop riffs, disjointed, in a group meeting of Schizophrenia Anonymous; and Pauling's ceaseless claims about a vitamin for every twisted thought.

I can't promise what I can't deliver. I tried for over fifteen thousand office hours. I'm not so sure now that it doesn't make as much trouble as it undoes. Something has happened to the psychotherapy that I used to think was a good idea. Or has the something happened to me?

My cardiologist came to see me after Kapilloff left. A line of physicians in white coats was behind the Great Man like a parade of penguins. After the demonstration of his warm bedside manner, he told me that my EKG showed that the damage might not be permanent. Further tests would settle the issue. The group nodded.

I conduct this procession on the psychiatry service. The professor is followed by the associate professor, the assistant professor, instructors, chief residents, junior residents, interns, senior medical students, junior medical students, and then the nurses. The chief nurse walks with the professor. It's a horizontal display of a vertical arrangement. Hanging on the words of the Chief, members of the entourage confirm his thoughts with agreeable detail and looks of enthrallment. An occasional arab responds with an unblinking stare. If the Chief is in the mood, he picks up the invitation for skirmish. After the rebel is acknowledged with a "Doctor, you don't look like you understand," the starer answers with a quote from an ancient or esoteric journal. "Isn't it true that the *South African Journal of Parasitology* at the turn of the century published a report of a worm mimicking the signs of an arteriosclerotic occlusion of the left anterior descending artery?" Male hormones surging, secretly triumphant, overly earnest, the dissident physician waits, excited. The old man scores with a roundhouse: "In the *Medical Jour-*

nal of Australia last month there was another case of such a worm. The first was in eighteen forty-four. If you'll look at the record, you'll see that the T waves are different if the agent is a parasite. Since you have the interest, why not report the details of all the world's cases to us at next week's rounds?" The group hides its grins.

As I lie in bed and watch this centuries-old medical ritual, measuring cerebral phalluses, a game of territoriality and dominance that claimed so much of my brain and body, it suddenly looks trivial. From a concertmaster's chair in a symphony to a first-string position in football, why must so much of what people like me try to do be driven by the vectors of power? Our society has made the pattern so exalted, and it's so primitive. The sequence is stereotyped. To see the Great Man. To hold him in reverent respect. To be noticed by him. To be admired, loved, and taught by him. To kill him. To eat his heart. To become him. To spend the rest of one's days awaiting the next round of murders by the obsequious; eyes downcast and head bowed until gaining entrance to the tent of the commander, they wound and kill. Followed by lifelong danger dreams of retaliation. Keeping loins guarded in lecture halls and ward rounds.

The tribal rites of the middle brain. Fights over mates; killing the old and weakened leader. Fearful respect for the new and shiny-coated champion. Some say that much of this has disappeared in this civilized day of empathy, restraint, a corporate life of egalitarian group process. Nonsense. The scars invoked by the middle brain have moved from the realm of the blindness of a club-fractured skull or an upper limb grown back together at an awkward angle to a world of middle-age depression, ulcers, strokes, coronaries, alcoholism, sleeping-pill addiction, amphetamine habits, and suicide. The winners die first.

From where I am now, the whole thing looks atavistic, self-destructive, and dumb. The game, like the black whip of last night's perversion, loses its erotic excitement in the cool, clear light of day.

It's been twenty-four years of tough work. Nights and days. Bleeding an investment from my family for which I would live to pay. The activities got more complex, less directly related to pure scientific search and clinical work, but absolutely necessary for their conduct. I have a research team of sixteen. The job description is complex: artist, artisan, businessman, politician, money raiser, hypnotizer, group dynamics leader, hustler, disciplinarian, mother, father, brother, seducer, cheerleader, lover, bullshitter, and killer. Quiet moments are spent doubting. In a coronary intensive care unit, what was a heroic effort to land a man on the brain becomes a personal exercise of a power game, a concerto for middle brain and heart muscle.

There must be a scientific advance, industrial productivity, and care giving without such corporate madness. Futurology, so dependent on middle-brain paranoia during the epochs of reference for Darwin, Marx, and Freud, is now being done by the calm electricity of a computer program—guessing what's going to happen next in every sphere far better than our psychopathology has ever allowed. All paranoia does these days is make us sick. Soon it will destroy the world.

"I've read some of your papers in preparation for the workshop. If you don't mind, I'll sit here and we can talk over lunch." The short, thick, dark, intense middle-aged man in a red outdoorsman shirt sat down in spite of my frown. I was teaching current concepts in the biology of depression to a hundred professors of psychiatry. I was now one of those pretentious know-nothings whom I called Great Men when I was in medical school. Behind my visitor's head was a view of a high mountain peak that still wore a snow skirt in July.

"By all means." I waved him into the seat. It was not long ago, and I had reached the end of my capacity to pretend. A trial lawyer's facility with rapid rearrangements of fact to fit the needs of the moment grated against a small but still honest voice inside me that wanted to say, "Not yet; we're not ready to say. For God's sake, I don't know. Maybe I'll never know. Leave me alone. I tried."

"In nineteen sixty-eight, you boys suggested that nor-epinephrine was the red of your model. Later that dopamine was the red. Now people are saying that both of them are the red. In a space of six years it's turned around three times. What shall I tell my medical students?" He was angry.

His questions descended on me like wet weight. Maybe the sparkling mountain air, the sunny lightness, the massive statements of the blankets of evergreens and quaking poplars on bold mountains made our words about natural processes seem more impotent than usual. I was to teach the witch doctors a cosmology of which I knew little because they needed a belief to be less fearful of their medicines. There was a snap in my head. A quiet click to the position marked OFF on a dialysis machine by a patient with kidney failure who could no longer live every minute with the toxic feeling of flu.

"Would you believe that I don't know? That no one knows? That maybe in a few years . . .?"

"Come on! I didn't come all this way to hear that. I can't tell that to my students. You think that I won't understand. You're purposely . . ."

"I'm telling you that all we can do is speculate. The students must be made to understand that our understanding about the brain hasn't come to full fruition. We'll know more soon."

"Didn't you hear me? The students I teach need to give drugs to their patients. They can't wait for you fellows." I remembered that I used to think that when the Great Men said they didn't know, they were holding out. The red-shirted professorpecker wasn't going to quit.

"Make it simple. Draw a diagram. I know that everything isn't known. I'll copy the diagram and teach it to the students."

Maybe it was the altitude. Maybe it was because I'm over forty. Maybe it was because my depression had already begun. I got up from the table and threw my napkin down on the plate, and before I rushed to my room, I heard myself saying, tears behind my eyes, "Don't you understand? There isn't any knowing and there aren't any Great Men to tell us. We made them up. God damn it, can't you see? I can't be a Great Man. There aren't any."

At a dinner for us, John Lilly's piercing eyes and sardonic grin were the same as I remembered when Uncle Al took Mary and me to visit his laboratories over twenty years ago. He seemed a little heavier, a little older, but still gave an impression of being full of efficient energy. He still spoke tersely, in an abbreviated and cryptic style, about the man in the brain, but now it was in different words. The differences in form of the conversations, twenty years apart, were enormous. Neuroanatomy had changed into Sufi spaces, logical positivism into mysticism, left-brain tautologies into right-brain hallucinations, competitive tests of intellect into an unterritorial benignity, cynical assaults on the politics of science into a quiet resignation about the facts of commerce, from a defensive macho into a compassionate reserve. He knew the land I had come from; did he know where I could go? Had he found a new road or an old one with a new street sign? Was the Lilly of Cal Tech and the National Institutes of Health the same or different from the Lilly of Oscar Ichazo's calisthenics? Was he a refugee scout back from a place beyond the land of neurobiology who could describe a new trail, or a traveling word salesman with fresh bunting for suicide? Was Lilly me?

He still looks a bit like an Eastern preppie or a business-school student from Princeton. His manner, that of an engineering professor, adds credibility to his pronouncements. When selling spook stuff, appearance and style play important roles. When Leary took LSD and tried to sell outer-space real estate, he was turned into a broken political prisoner. When Lilly did it, the publishers paid him handsome advances. His camouflage of objectivity made gentler his transitions from the electrical activity of the brain, through the mind of the dolphin, to the center of his cyclone. It's a search for salvation seen often among explorers of the nervous system. It gets more naked with advancing years.

It's long been known that doctors choose specialties that have personal meaning. My friend with one kidney is an internist who works with renal disease. The father of my friend the cardiologist died in his early forties with a coronary. I know two neurologists with multiple sclerosis. I became a psychiatrist to learn to deal with my own craziness and to cure an unpredictably moody father. Almost all medical students have an inordinate fear of death and think that their degree will make them safe on the other side of the counter.

For Lilly and me, knowing how the brain machine works is getting to the central switchboard of reality—the hope is that fear, pain, and despair can be changed by the simple process of changing their codes. The brain promises such opportunities. This witchcraft doesn't require objective examples of alchemy, but the sculpting of seeing, hearing, and thought. The brain is a rolled-up record of man. When the city of the head becomes the flat emptiness of desert on mornings of depression, it's reassuring for us brain people to know that other worlds lie waiting—if one can find them.

Is Lilly a Whitehead or an Ouspensky? His solipsistic, hallucinogen-facilitated head burrowing into brain and space has the appearance of a rational search. I know of that sound, its disguises, its path near suicide. I too have looked to the brain's cortical mantle, the moonless sky, and the empty space inside that comes from hours of the mantra for a meteoric magism of salvation.

Twenty years ago, after showing Mary and me a monkey brain broadcast through electronic trickery—a Las Vegas collage of lights—he spoke of information storage and retrieval, a system of pleasure and pain, and an integrative schema made of chalk on a blackboard. He mouthed a theory of brain function in which an unknown whole is divided into several unknown parts. He moved around, pointing to the equipment whose hours of humming justified his statements. I could tell he knew it wasn't working. He was bored.

So he went to sea to talk to mammals who had escaped back to the water. He taught us that dolphins speak in two languages, have bigger and more complex brains than man, and, wisely, are secretive about their knowledge. He listened for a long time before giving up the idea that a dolphin knew better than we did why we get up in the morning. He closed his laboratory in the Caribbean, announcing that it wasn't to quit the search, but to begin to find out.

Lilly casts doubts on my brain escape by making a path that looks circular. It seems to have brought him back to the beginning. Is he like I am now, so buried in himself, so tripped by his own feet, that the discovery of other than himself is a logistical impossibility? No matter how logical the arguments, no matter how high-flown the terminology? Listen as hard as I might, I hear only hopelessness and mime. Is that what's left for me?

Lilly is a cult figure. His *Center of the Cyclone* rang people's heads and now serves as a guide.

His books and life had taught me about a new job, that of professional magician. Do I want it? He's paid to lift our perspective out of the doldrums. Of course, that was his job description twenty years ago, but the institutional arrangements are different. Card tricks about how our heads work through out-of-the-body energies. At first so credible as to fool himself; now, knowing, he uses the claims about the brain (now called spirit, cosmos, spaces, and places) like so many torches and clubs.

We professionals are paid for such services by the hour. Rentals on a self that have become less with every lease. Finally, only the fantasy of occupancy can be honestly billed because what was good is all used up and what is left, if not hidden, can do in our would-be tenants through a creeping paralysis of will, of spark, of being, of life. The quiet and unobtrusive suicide of a withered, childless, sick, and humdrum widower cannot be prevented with new hope by a whore whose hole was used with such desperation as to have worn away the rim, leaving the edge of human feeling near the disappearing boundary of the last measurement and infinity.

I heard recently that the *poules de luxe* of Paris are striking for health benefits and retirement. It would certainly make our later years less insecure: Lilly's, mine, and those of the cardiologist who just left. But I don't think that the insurance plans will pay off in a magic strong enough to carry us and our patients to another hope.

The delusions of my first cycle are at an end and to continue by faking it isn't going to be enough.

TEN

Out of danger, I was eager to move on, but didn't know how. I took short walks, but for the rest of the time it was two square yards of bed. I writhed to get loose.

Drug befuddled, I rolled to a cooler part of the bed and turned the pillow to get a fresh start. My head talked in ponderous words, careful yet bizarre. Working on my problems in murky somnolence, thoughts became things, things became thoughts, and the machinery ran on.

In moments of clarity I reviewed my solutions and laughed: I'd start a bar and play jazz piano; run away to Bermuda and start a renewal center for burned-out psychotherapists with daily running, poetry reading, mantras, and making love with the professional staff of big-breasted blond women who gushed love juice like fountains and smiled broadly in their pleasure; create a mania molecule because up is young and old is down—brain hormones failing. In my sleep I went to Rumania and talked to that woman who gave injections and found that her rejuvenated oldies slept only four hours a night and were manic the rest of the time. I concluded that chemical mania was the fountain of youth and I turned in bed to fresh and cool territory to expound the new theory.

Lying there, I conducted neurochemical research, metaphysical reaches, and remembered my poetry lesson, the words of the insurance executive: "The poem of the

mind in the act of finding / What will suffice." Wallace
Stevens was sane and made a living. I needed a fresh place
to do the same. Moving in bed, the voice droned on. I
worked so hard between the shots and pills, I couldn't
waste the time. It's hard to tell how what happened next
started. I don't know how long it lasted and I can't say
what it was. In *Humboldt's Gift*, Bellow's guru, Dr.
Scheldt, pointed out to him in his moment of crisis that
consciousness in the self creates a false distinction between
subject and object.

SAM! SAM! THAT'S ENOUGH RUMINATING.

"What . . ." I heard the voice against an eerie hum
of an electrical motor. It had been my best day. After my
electrocardiogram came back normal, I was moved to a
private room. Euphoric, I settled down for my first night's
sleep without the fear of imminent death. The hum, per-
sistent, was familiar—like the sound I heard in my childhood when my father, caught in an unstoppable seizure of
anger, cornered and lectured me. I watched his face turn
into a plastic Stalin doll with a soundless, moving mouth.
The hum masked his words. Then, as now, things were
unreal. The low illumination in the hall made vague
shadows from the room's furniture. There was a silver
nimbus around everything. It could have been night-
marish except for the unmistakable feeling of buoyancy.
I lay on my back staring at the ceiling.

MIDDLE BRAIN, COLOR POOL, SECOND CYCLE, DARWIN,
MARX, FREUD, WILD FLOWERS, TESTICLE, PETE ROZELLE,
THELONIOUS MONK. I HAVEN'T HEARD SUCH COMPLICATED
NEUROTICISM SINCE ALAN WATTS EXPLAINED HIS ALCO-
HOLISM.

No mistaking it, a female voice, and it sounded tough.
One of those lady athletes, hard thighs, developed arm
muscles with the vaccination, who squeeze you so hard
with their legs you get blood in the kidneys and have to
sleep late. Out of a dark corner it came, the same place I
used to hear voices when I was little and hiding my head

under the covers. I get out of death row and the harassment starts—my brain won't leave me alone.

COME ON, SAM, THE DETACHMENT YOU SAY YOU WANT SO MUCH WON'T GROW OUT OF ALL THAT CRAP YOU'VE BEEN THINKING.

The diction was precise; the voice sounded authoritative. She was probably a good volleyball player. I felt an irritation. I had had enough trouble. "Who are you? Why are you calling me that name?"

STOP ASKING QUESTIONS. THERE'S NO SAFE WAY TO GET TO DETACHMENT ANY MORE THAN THERE IS TO DEATH OR INSANITY. THINGS LIKE THAT HAVE NO CONTINUITY. THEY'RE REACHED WITH A LEAP, NOT A LADDER. YOU PARANOID JEWS WANT GUARANTEES. YOU NEVER WANT TO DO ANYTHING DIFFERENT—JUST THE SAME THING OVER AND OVER AGAIN WITH DIFFERENT ADJECTIVES FROM YOUR PSYCHOANALYSTS. YOU WERE TOO SCARED TO DIVE OFF A TEN-FOOT BOARD WHEN YOU WERE FOURTEEN, AND HERE YOU ARE, FROZEN AGAIN. ANY MINUTE YOU'RE GOING TO TAKE OUT THAT PEN YOU CALL LIVING AND WRITE A LECTURE ON THE NEUROCHEMISTRY OF THE FEAR OF CHANGE.

That is a nasty lady. Who is she to talk to me that way, so contemptuously superior? After ejaculatio precox I could understand, but why now?

YOU KNOW WHY NOW. DIDN'T YOU TELL KAPILLOFF YOU HAD A NEW IDEA?

Yes.

WHAT WAS IT?

I was going to change my name. To be a new person.

BIG SOPHISTICATED THINKER ABOUT HUMAN BEHAVIOR AND YOU THINK CHANGING THE NAME CHANGES THE PERSON?

I know it sounds superficial. Cassius Clay changed his name to Muhammad Ali; Lew Alcindor, to Kareem Abdul-Jabbar; Bobby Moore, to Ahmad Rashad, and they said it worked.

WELL, HERE IT IS. SAM SHAMBHALA. DR. SAM SHAMBHALA.

Who?

DR. SAM SHAMBHALA. YOUR NEW NAME. NOW, YOU
COWARD, GET OUT OF BED AND GET DRESSED. YOU'VE GOT A
NEW LIFE TO LIVE.

It sounded like a good idea even in a bitchy voice. I
had promised Kapilloff that I would talk to him before
doing anything, but this was different. I flipped back the
covers and dangled my feet over the side of the bed. Nothing hurt. I felt the best I'd felt in months. Out the window
of my eighth-floor room I saw the twinkling lights of the
city's hills in the distance and the freeway's bright raceway
just below. It must be a hysterical fugue. If it were a drug
or brain injury I wouldn't have my recent memory. If it
were an attack of schizophrenia I would be illogical. It
must be the state that actors and other fakes get into when
they're stressed. I never thought of myself as one of those
fainting, dramatic, hysterical types . . . yet I do like to
perform in front of audiences. Maybe this was a whole
new dimension of my personality. . . . I would have to . . .

CAN'T YOU STOP THAT BULLSHIT FOR ONE MINUTE? DO
YOU SHRINKS HAVE TO ORGANIZE EVERYTHING? WHO CARES
ABOUT YOUR DIAGNOSIS? GET DRESSED!

Her voice was stronger than my doubts. She probably
had my good at heart. I found my clothes in the closet and
got dressed. I sat in a chair and waited further instructions.
I felt so full of energy.

OUT THE DOOR! WHEN YOU LEAVE OLD THINGS, NEW
THINGS BEGIN TO HAPPEN BY THEMSELVES. YOU DON'T HAVE
TO CARRY YOUR OLD LIFE IN A BAG LIKE THE REFUGEES DID
WITH THEIR DIAMONDS. MOVE!

To go empty-handed into a new world! With the lack
of elegance in her symbolism, she probably had not been
an English major. I stepped tentatively out the door of
the room. A slight young man in thick glasses, blue flannel
shirt, and jeans told me to stand on the line, look backward, and grab the right strut of the red chair as soon as
it hit me behind my knees. The hum turned out to be the
pulley motor of a chair lift. I swung free of the building

and found myself rising slowly up a mountain—the wind and the motor became one, and the lightness I was feeling was everywhere. Below, wild flowers, firs, and thick green brush looked radiant in the strong sun. Behind and below me, the hospital and the city were retreating in the distance.

THE FIRST STOP IS THE SALK INSTITUTE.

The man at the landing grabbed my hand and helped me off. I walked on a path toward a small white building through a grove of long, straight firs like pencils in a rack. Smart lady! Jonas Salk was also a refugee from a death in the first cycle. The triumphant swell of his early career soon turned to withering pain when he lost his battle with Sabin. He lived now in the emotional alienation from fellow scientists that results from early celebrity and jealous politics. He was the sixth best-loved man in a poll of the world and lived alone in his institute on Elba. His second-cycle life was in the boundary land between population biology and the social sciences. I walked through the open double door into a large formal garden. Greek columns, fountains, and statuary were in the inner court of the building. Large male and female bodies in cold white marble stared at me in ancient sightlessness. Smallish and in long, white, cotton robes, Jonas walked contemplatively in sandals with his refined woman's hands clasped behind him.

"Jonas!" He stopped his stroll and looked up with a smile.

"It's in the genes of all things that live in groups.'"

"What?"

"The bacterial growth curves of cultures in my laboratory do what each of us does in our lives and what each civilization has done in the history of the world. In our early period we grow gradually; in our middle period we develop at an accelerating rate; in our late period we stop growing." He talked with a quiet intensity. A slight and graceful man, balding, he had the youthful look of new adventure. We walked slowly side by side, and I clasped my hands behind me like his. "When growth stops, the bacterial culture has to be transplanted or it begins to contaminate itself with its own wastes—leading to mutant forms which have no mobility and can't multiply. The whole species gets sick and disappears unless you can put it into a new place. The trouble with moving people like you, Sam, is that there's a lot of fear."

"Why not stay and make things better? Some kind of renewal, a rediscovery?"

"It doesn't work, Sam. Things pile up. Fixed ideas, pollution, anomie, aging, rheumatoid arthritis, divorce, cancer, insanity—most people will accept any sickness to avoid the risk of moving."

"So what's your treatment?"

"Explantation. A surgical procedure. Move to a new place. Out of worn and tired thoughts."

"Into where? Can't you see, that's the problem? Into where?"

"Once you make the move you'll learn how silly that question is. You sound as afraid of empty space as you were of the dark. There will be more and more richness— but you'll never find out until it's too late to turn back."

As I took the dirt path to the next chair lift, I wondered whether he was right. How many modern metaphysics manufacturers make their living with this salesman's doublethink: you have to care but if you care you're attached, so detach and be free, but care enough to become a trainer in our new religion? The Zen practitioners do it with the paradox of one hand clapping. How can I know?

The next lift took me over rock slides and the fallen trunks of dead trees, lying scattered over the downhill slopes like soldiers fallen in battle.

THERE'S A MAN WHO KNOWS. IF YOU DON'T BELIEVE ME, YOU CAN CERTAINLY BELIEVE SALK.

Listen, Lady, whoever you are, unfortunately I too have a salesman's brain. If you don't like the color of the suit I'm selling, I change the lights. We quick-change artists of the intellect lie with many truths.

MAYBE YOU WILL HAVE TO DIE.
Wait a minute, God damn it. I'm just talking. I mean, these are the doubts. Do you want me to hide them? I ask you, where does an Armenian go to buy rugs for his house?
YOU MAKE THINGS SO CONVOLUTED THAT IT'S A WONDER YOU CAN FIND YOUR FLY WHEN IT'S TIME TO PEE. YOU'RE GIVING ME A HEADACHE.

Intern's Note: Called to patient's room by charge nurse at 10:25 and found bed empty, closet door open, clothes gone, hospital gown on floor. No one saw patient leave the room. Kapilloff notified. No next of kin indicated on chart. Nurses will search. They say he was in high spirits when last seen after dinner.

Rosencrantz

I was feeling more exhilarated the higher the chair lift climbed. After getting off the lift at the second level, I walked a path of bright green moss through a clump of tall evergreens, cool, dark earth underfoot. Then suddenly I emerged into the hot, burning sunlight of a desert. In the distance I saw the deep reds, slate grays, and greens of the foothills of the mountains around Santa Fe. I walked on a crudely paved street of pebbles lined on one side with adobe huts. The sky was an endless blue, the sun a naked torch. A faded street sign said Canyon. Through the windows of the deserted houses I saw leather-latched wooden furniture, potbellied stoves, Indian earthenware, and blankets. From the last house on the short street emerged a familiar, tall, somewhat corpulent and balding man with a full gray beard and granny glasses—he was rushing toward me in a long red-and-white-striped apron and carrying a baker's tray. I smelled freshly baked bread. He seemed proud.

"It came out perfectly. Ground wheat, molasses, a little yeast, salt and pepper, and two lids of homegrown grass. I did everything myself. Can you believe it? Here, have some." He tore off a corner, and I put it in my mouth. I loved the earth taste but didn't like the gritty feeling.

"See where I baked it." We walked on the red-clay brick path behind the house and I saw a large adobe oven used for firing pots. I sat down on a broken rocker, and he joined me on a stool. The sun's warmth felt good. He explained.

"It started the first day of football training camp. As a rookie, I kept watching the old pros to see what the game was really like. I was a tough blocking back in college, and during my last year I won the student body presidency, but that's a lot different than getting drafted by the White House and playing for a coaching staff like Dick Nixon and George Allen."

"You're John Ehrlichman! You look so different." He was not only fatter and had a beard, there was a softness.

"In my old life I was John Ehrlichman. Now I'm Ramdas Hash." He clasped his hands together as though in prayer and chanted unintelligibly.

"What are you doing? This is the last place in the world I would have guessed you'd be. I always thought that you were, well, down on the counterculture."

"The only door out of my old place led here. I had to escape. Scared, in debt, ready for jail. Then I met a little girl with stringy blond hair in a bar in Taos. One thing led to another and before we got in bed she gave me this funny-looking cigarette. She said it would make everything feel better—and last longer. I figured I was going to jail anyway and had lots of time to think about it, so I just smoked it. I can't begin to tell you what happened. It took me hours to come and when I did, it was wonderful. The little girl smiled at my amazement. After she fell asleep I took a long walk in the moonlight—thinking about how things had happened for me. I couldn't believe how tiny, harmless steps, one after another, took me so far away from myself without even knowing it."

"What do you mean?" That lady was producing real miracles. First Salk and now John Ehrlichman as a hippie!

"As I was saying, it starts in training camp. You learn what it's going to take. A hold, a clip, then a little dirt in their faces; pretty soon you overamp on speed, stamp their hands with your cleats. At first you spend your nights thinking about it. Do you want to play that kind of game? Do you want to be that kind of person? Give up all your college idealism? Then you get hooked on the Big Dream that justifies everything: winning. You'll make the fans happy for a whole week after the game—mostly poor slobs who have to do what they're told the rest of the time. When you win, they win. You do real good for the guys who own the hot dog concession. Winning fills the stadium and the owner of the parking lots has lots of kids to feed. There's a *new* idealism. Showing the fans that we could deliver the Camelot that Joe Namath only promised—before he was assassinated in Texas."

"Wait a minute, aren't you mixing a bunch of stuff?"

He spoke in a beatific calm. "Then the mind rises. The squeeze comes from all sides and your brain comes out the top like toothpaste. It isn't the same anymore. You can't see the damage you're doing. Excited, you go down on the special teams and put their starting center out of the game; you clothesline their chicken-shit wide receiver and can feel a thrill. You step on the throwing hand of the quarterback; you and a buddy finish a linebacker's knee with a high-low crackback. Then the night arrives for the winners. You sit with Allen, Nixon, and Pete Rozelle Himself at the Royal Table in the middle of a half-circle of flag-draped round tables at the annual Super Bowl banquet. You join Pete, Mrs. Lombardi, and all the owners in singing songs about owning all the politicians and news media in the nation and throwing half-eaten chicken legs to a chorus line of black offensive tackles dancing on their knees and singing spirituals. History is being made, and you're part of it."

"How bad did it get before you left?"

"It didn't feel bad. It all felt normal. A chairman of a department has to feed his faculty. You have to get contracts, grants, negotiate with bureaucracies, fire the unproductive, threaten, cajole, and high-pressure. You have no time to do the caring things that brought you into the business in the first place. Patient care is rushed, students are ignored; there's no time to nourish the spirit. You build a successful academic machine and it runs efficiently, ruthlessly. Only the hitters survive. If a wide receiver doesn't have the courage to stick his nose into the middle and publish, you put him on waivers and release the assistant professor for a hundred-buck claiming fee."

I could feel it. The hard, cold, rigid edge of duty rubbing against a nervous feeling of caring. I had a job to do! God, what terrible words. How much mayhem has been inflicted upon the world with that rationale. "I think you're being unnecessarily negative. I really do."

"So what are you doing here? Aren't you looking for a way out?" He watched my face.

I needed time to think. Salk on contaminated cultures and now Ehrlichman on kindness. "Ramdas, of course. Red, middle brain, Freud, anger, fear, my father, and pieces of penis got all mixed together and clogged my arteries. I was a physiological inadequate—when I did my job I got sick. Finally they put me in a death house and wouldn't let me out until I thought about it. I don't know what I'm going to do."

"Here, take the bread. The window out is baked inside."

Attending Physician's Note: Called a little before 10:30 by Dr. Rosencrantz who reported that the patient had disappeared from his room sometime after dinner. He's been emotionally labile, with periods of manic expansiveness and other times of depression and withdrawal. There is the possibility of suicide. He seemed in good spirits this afternoon after learning about his negative EKG, but every effort should be made to find him. His moods change quickly. His ex-wife was called and has no knowledge of his whereabouts. No one in the lobby or emergency room saw him leave. The cab company has received no calls, and he didn't have a car at the hospital. The cardiologist has been alerted. The hospital staff will continue the search.

Kapilloff

What a magical ride! On the third stage of the lift there could be no doubt. The higher I went, the lighter I felt. It was as though I was dropping all kinds of weight. That lady with the voice knew what she was doing. The wind, now blowing harder and colder, was invigorating. The empty chairs ahead swayed in the breeze. Looking back, the city had become a postage stamp with topography. In front of me were rugged peaks and a thinning density of trees. Far below, a river ran along a road: two parallel ribbons, one a gray-white, the other a sparkling silver in the sun. I began to tingle with anticipation.

SO IT FEELS GOOD. HAVE YOU LEARNED ANYTHING?

I started to answer and then there weren't any words. It was all feeling. A sensation of incipient freedom. A tunnel digger seeing a tiny sliver of light ahead. A swell in the chest. I wanted it so bad and was afraid to trust.

YOU'RE AFRAID TO SAY IT. YOU THINK IF YOU ACKNOWLEDGE SOMETHING GOOD IT WILL GO AWAY. SUPERSTITIOUS CHILDREN OF IMMIGRANT JEWS ARE ALL THE SAME. SAY IT! HEAR YOURSELF SAY IT!

Who needed to follow that lady like a slave? I was getting fed up with all her bossiness. I don't care if she *was* helping. I was led off the third stage of the lift by a big blond woodsman who pointed in the direction of a small wooden building marked Ski Patrol: Dr. Armand Hammer, President. I used to think he was head of a company that made baking soda. Recently I learned he was an enormously adroit tradesman—the volume sales of fine art and a Russian pencil monopoly. His biggest success, Occidental Petroleum, had been bought and built after he was fifty.

"Whom shall I say is here?" A tall secretary with

white streaked hair and silver-rimmed glasses hanging around her neck on a chain was his only staff member.

"Dr. Sam Shambhala."

"Are you here about Dr. Hammer's plans for a chain of hospitals, the new pharmaceutical plant, or his international scientific consulting firm?"

"Well, actually, I . . ."

"Maybe it has to do with Occidental. I think he's obligated the company to supply medical expertise to the OPEC countries."

"No, it has nothing to do with that."

"What can I say it's in reference to?"

"His midlife crisis."

"Dr. Shambles . . ."

"Shambhala."

"Dr. Shambhala, are you being funny? You know that Dr. Hammer is in his late seventies."

I began to explain when an office door burst open and a fast-moving, rotund little man with a red face and white hair came toward me with an extended hand.

"Did I hear the name Shambhala?"

"Yes."

"I have a message for you from Thomas Carlyle." He and Benjamin Franklin thought they needed to tell people how not to be lazy. I needed that advice now like another disease. We sat in two chairs in the inner office in front of his huge desk. His wood-paneled office was lined with citations.

"I believe that you have some special knowledge of . . ."

"Before I was fifty, I was doing fine. Wall Street thought I was pretty brave, opening up new markets like Russia, selling Rembrandts at Macy's. But that was nothing. After I was fifty, something happened."

"Something happened?" I was on the edge of my chair.

"Ever since Dr. Joseph Heller used that phrase in his textbook of geriatrics, I've loved it. Something happened.

My fear went away. I stopped caring so desperately. One day without warning there were no more night sweats or jaw grinding. I sat down at nickel-a-point rummy at the Friars without an apparatus up my sleeve; I carried cash instead of traveler's checks; I stopped washing my dick with alcohol after going to bed with a new woman. That's when the Occidental success began. I had a whole new career. No more cowardly, courageous rushes into business deals, no more claims of omnipotence. I just wait until the time is right and everything happens by itself. It's also a hell of a lot more fun."

"What did it?"

"Surrendering. Giving up. When I began to feel the power of my surrender, I knew I had found a new world."

"How can you call it giving up when you got so much more productive?" I shuddered at the thought that he was going to give me a lecture on the harmony of opposites. I can barely hang onto my own gyrations.

"Ah, that's the point. It's the easy doing of giving up. It flows. After your fear goes away, there isn't any more work. Just activity." He picked up a manila folder with sheets full of numbers and returned to his side of the desk and began to check them with a red pen.

As I left the little brown wooden building, I saw that there was a fourth lift. I walked toward it over a bed of crushed red rock.

Attending Cardiologist's Note: Spoke with Kapilloff again shortly after midnight. He informed me that the patient had been missing from his room all evening. He is believed to be in the hospital. Current cardiac status reviewed. Since EKG and serum enzymes are now normal and there has been no pain, I don't think there is any immediate danger. Would have preferred that he return to ambulatory status more gradually. Will be available by phone should the need arise.

Sullivan

Night Nursing Supervisor's Note: All doctors notified. Search of eighth floor led to the discovery of patient's pants, shirt, shoes, and socks on a couch in the TV room at 4:15 A.M. Still no sign of patient. Search will continue. Incident report has been filled out and will be given to the hospital director in the morning.

Cartwright

ELEVEN

Riders were required to abandon all they owned before ascending the final stage. The only sounds were the hum of the pulley motor and a high-pitched whine as the cable cut the cold edge of the wind. From the high platform I saw miles into an ocean of mountaintops, dark grays and blues, textured by deep glaucous patches of the still snow-wet evergreens of late summer. Sometimes rolling in the shadows of the windblown clouds, mostly the waves stood frozen. So little, yet we mites survive. A set of brain sparks and all this is seen. I took off my clothes and wrapped myself in a blue blanket.

YOU UNDERSTAND THE CONDITIONS?

The man said to leave my things at the bottom.

YOU'VE LEFT EVERYTHING?

Wife, career, home, reputation, hobbies, commitments, values, beliefs, everything I could think of . . . except, except my sons. I'm waiting a little on that. Don is nineteen and though he's on his own, I think he still needs me a little. And with Ross, my fourteen-year-old, I have a few rounds that even the Greeks thought were necessary.

SHAMBHALA, AFTER ALL YOUR CONFESSIONS YOU STILL CAN'T FACE THE TRUTH. DO YOU THINK YOU WANT TO STAY STUCK TO HELP THEM? THAT LINEBACKING NONSENSE IS AN

137

EXCUSE FOR YOUR OWN FEAR. YOU PITHLESS DO-GOODERS AL-
WAYS GIVE YOUR CHILDREN AS THE REASON YOU DON'T HAVE
THE COURAGE TO GROW.

You're a vicious bitch. A bull dike psychiatrist sticking her nose into . . . moving away from Don was like
tearing off a limb . . . how would you know? . . . I almost
killed myself . . . go give advice to somebody else. . . .

YOU'LL HAVE TO SEE THE OCTOPUS.

I stumbled as the chair swept me up. It was moving
quickly, pulled by a cable strung along a rising, sharp
ridge of the mountain; the steep sides plunged downward
for hundreds of feet. The height brought a yawning, fearful feeling to my groin. My heart was racing in dread and
excitement all at once, as I sat helpless. In the distance,
standing above the rock waves, was a tall, broad, pleated
side of a dark mountain peak, the highest, its skirt edged
in snow. *There* was a bold statement of being. Not on
trial, not trying to do it properly, not trying to be pretty,
to be loved. God, how painful it had been with Don. Cold
wind howling against the ridge edge, blanket drawn
around me for warmth, the red lift chair moved me on in
my journey. The triadic knot, Don, Mary, and I, had been
too tight.

Tall, slim, and with his mother's handsome face, he
shared a verbal facility that neither of us trusted. Mary
and I brought him into the game too early. Freak amounts
of adult sophistry poured from him with the ease of an
athletic skill learned young. Don and I disguised our love
with intellectually tough and satirical dialogue. I saw the
same contempt that I felt toward my father's way, but with
too much intimacy between us for him to be angry without crippling guilt. He knew too much, too quick. I
helped take away the necessary adolescent blindness for
him to use in the clean and righteous hate of the father.
I had shared my human foibles as though doing so was
democratic—calling my cowardice honesty and justifying
my actions with the latest edition of *Summerhill*.

As parents, my generation chose the path of mutual

search and befuddlement rather than serving our biological role as strong, transitional icons for our children. It was to protect ourselves from their rage—the same rage we felt for our parents, who were more secure in their knowing. It didn't work. Using intellectualized tentativeness, we chose a try for their friendship when their respect was the required piece of ethology. What chaos there would be in the cat family if the parent tiger, in place of the cuffs and temporary starvation necessary to teach the young to hunt, gave adolescent group therapy in a protected cave stocked with meat.

The ordained structures of youthful learning—the wallness of walls and the roofness of roofs—only later in *my* life became the shifting *mise en scène* of Pirandello. My elder son was in the 1960s wave of kids who knew this immediately. We, whose slower rate of development allowed time for the maturation of the solid features of mental organization, could hardly wait to break the news of intrinsic flimsiness—telling the secret would make us quick friends. We explained the rule against swearing on school playgrounds as culturally determined and open for negotiations using tracts from the sociology of Erving Goffman.

We loved their politics. We hated our fathers too. We knew what it feels like to want to kill them; our strivings for the safety of the top came from our fears of revenge. Our nervous tics and psychoanalytic monologues came from the spillage. Our heterosexual stealth and sneakiness, our too-fast or absent orgasms, our sports cars, our conglomerates, our new treatments for cancer and schizophrenia, all grew from our dealings with strong and normal human emotions. Yet we made up talk about how trivial it all was so they wouldn't be envious or feel little.

We deified their deviations as acts of creativity and took them for leaders. We relaxed our efforts to maintain adult space and gave them free access to our showers and bickers. We failed in the job of protecting the child's space. The false belief was that all-wise children knew everything already. Had we forgotten, or did we ever know, that boundaries are mutual; that dropping the protection of our privacy was an invasion of *their* lives? As violating, as stimulus-strong, as selfishly adultrocentric as an Oedipal transgression, it was costumed in a new egalitarianism.

LISTEN TO THE WAILING! SUCH MUTILATING SELF-PITY! HOW YOU GUYS TAKE BASIC BIOLOGICAL PROCESSES AND SCREW THEM UP WITH YOUR FANCY TALK NEVER CEASES TO AMAZE ME.

I pulled the blue blanket around, not so much as a protection against the electrical edge of the cold wind, but because I needed boundaries. Rising, lighter, letting go, open, you're not the same. The you that you knew from your borders dissolves. The shrinking firs of the tree line, the strewn rocks, and the occasional bright splash of orange Indian brush and blue lupines disappeared in an enveloping mist.

Don was caught in the middle of our family's dissolution, unable to find his own calm place of work, verbally hardened by a three-year hobby of Synanon games (you don't have to be a junkie to learn their special lesson of interpersonal toughness). Competing with and yet rejecting the myths of two overachieving parents, seeing the living hypocrisy of a dying marriage coasting downhill in neutral, he had to get out. I became aware that the soft and shifting foundations of my belief had given him nothing to fight but my worsening disposition. Our battles, loud and vague, forced him from disdain to panic. I was busy erecting limits, long overdue, and was shocked when he pushed holes in those new drop curtains with ease. My every day's resolve ended in sleepless despair. I didn't know whether the accusations of poor judgment and sadism coming from Mary in our private talks were to correct for the crudeness of my belated and unpracticed efforts, or the vengeance of a hurt woman. I wanted her to leave us alone and yet demanded that she make sure I was doing no damage. It was all too late.

My knowledge, latent, was struggling for the surface like a blind mole, unused to the operations of the earth's surface. I at last had learned that the things I should have wanted him to do were the simple things, the required tasks of living. It was too late. Tangled in years of words, there was no simple way. Afraid of my feelings and untrusting of my judgments, I nonetheless demanded respect and respect for my limits. It was like trying to squeeze a six-foot eagle back into his egg. I felt, and felt that I looked, like Woody Allen playing Moses and was hurt by the laughter. My towering rages were a last-ditch effort and the organization of a guilty force that would soon try to kill me. It's a fact that a significant percentage of middle-aged men's suicides involve the relationships with their sons.

I took him with me on a lecture trip to Paris. On the second day, I returned to our hotel and found him sleeping. I sat by his bed and watched. Freed for a moment from dealing with his rain of probes and barbs, I saw a struggling, searching, suffering, desperate boy. Freed of the pain from his Albeean language and Japanese-copied insight, I could see his naivete. He was caught fighting battles that weren't his, left over from us, that were threatening to eat up the next time in his life as well as the last, and like the last, they would leave him nothing of his own but more of the vacuous irony and cynicism with which he had already been overdosed. The only thing there was left to do was to give him his freedom. Don would find a place to stay among strangers, go to school, learn the language, and at sixteen would be on his own in Paris. I felt the lift of a turn in the proper direction and the pain of loss so deep it couldn't be localized.

The night before I left him in Paris, I walled off a million Jewish-mother worries about good nutrition and medical care. We had dinner and took a long silent walk in the rain. Despair is too light a word. How does it feel when the most precious gift you can give to your most precious is your absence? We stood on the platform of a

Parisian underground railroad station, and my head hum, a loud buzzing, began. It got louder. A giant hand was on my back, pushing me onto the electrified third rail below. I was terrified. First, leaning, then sliding against the hand, then running, I hurried up the stairs onto the street. Don followed, confused.

It happened again. Don returned from France after several months. It was called a visit, but we both knew it was a time of assessment. He came in the middle of the last hopeless scream of our marriage. His head, now knowing freedom from this, ran amok. Ugly-tongued, critical, gossipy, contemptuous, assaultive, lying, humiliating, provoking, he ran roughshod over our feelings. He used up his bank account, his allowance, and tuition for the following year of school on night wildness with no explanation. My old urge to blame myself and apologize was strong, but some of my dying had led to the surrender of more of my delusions. This was the last opportunity to be parent. He was a rebellious seventeen-year-old with little experience in dealing with limits—not a savant or purveyor of a superior philosopy.

I took away his car and money. I put him on a plane. He would now have to make it on his own, even if he were to be sick or without food. It was time for him to test his claims. He's been in Paris since. On his own and doing well. Hungry and in the rain sometimes, but he became his own man. After that, my world was different. Parents who release their children surrender themselves as babies. The hug around the child-self, a posture for carrying the infant, has to become the open-arms acceptance of a new world. Or you die.

The morning after I sent him into his world, my bachelor apartment was cold and gray. The windows look down on a large beach rock, and that day a sea lion beckoned to me. I opened the window and rehearsed a fifty-foot fall. I stood at the open window for two hours— I called for help with an inside scream. Something, anything, to take away the pain. My grandfather's face, kind, concerned, but demanding, appeared. I was suddenly ashamed and closed the window.

HURRY. COME FIND ME. THERE'S NOT MUCH TIME LEFT.

The top of the lift was shrouded in fog. A narrow trail led away from the flat rock that served as a landing. I held my blanket tightly around me. The winding path was suspended in the mist, a ribbon in space. I saw a tall glass tank of bubbling water, six feet high and three feet in diameter, resting on a small platform in the middle of the walk. It took a few moments to realize that the collection of green and brown membranes was an octopus surrounded by a cloud of little white packets, hundreds, kept in constant motion by the stirring and brushing of her tentacles.

WATCH ME.

The woman's voice. A slick, oozy projection of my own brain, a giant neuron with many moving axons.

AS SOON AS I'M FINISHED TAKING CARE OF THESE CHILDREN, I CAN DIE. I'VE STOPPED EATING. FOR YEARS BIOLOGISTS HAVE TRIED TO KEEP ME ALIVE WITH LUSCIOUS LOBSTER, BUT I'M A ONE-CYCLE ANIMAL. THE SPERM SETS OFF THE WHOLE REFLEX. I STOP EATING AS SOON AS I DELIVER THESE LITTLE SACS AND USE THE REST OF MYSELF UP KEEPING THEM CLEAN. I DON'T HAVE TO STAY AROUND AND FIGHT WITH THESE KIDS WHEN THEIR HORMONES TELL ME TO FUCK OFF. IT DOESN'T MAKE ANY DIFFERENCE THAT MY PREGNANCY GAVE ME VARICOSE VEINS. I HAVE NO WORRIES ABOUT MY VAGINA GETTING DRIED OUT. AT LEAST THAT'S THE WAY IT WAS BEFORE PROFESSOR WODINSKY INVENTED A NEW OPERATION.

What's that?

IT'S CALLED A WODINSKY PROCEDURE. HE REMOVES THE OPTIC GLANDS AND THE APPETITE RETURNS. BY CHANGING THE BRAIN CHEMISTRY I CAN LIVE ANOTHER TIME. NOW I HAVE TO DECIDE WHETHER I WANT TO. YOUR WOMEN GET HYSTERECTOMIES, THEIR INTROITUS VAGINAE TIGHTENED, AND TAKE ESTROGEN TO BEGIN AGAIN. I DON'T KNOW WHAT YOU MEN DO.

I knew what I felt like doing.

What kind of suicide? A they'll-be-sorry suicide, with the fantasy of return to see the pain and guilt in the victims around the grave? The turn-off-the-pain-button suicide? I call on a blissful quiet when the head noise gets too jangly to tolerate, the nerves bleeding raw, the dull ache sharp enough to cut. The wither-to-dust-and-blow-away suicide? No more reason to do anything but go to sleep, a sleep that is soft as a pillow, cool as a breeze. Will it be a high suicide? Like the first rush of heroin, the peaking of an acid overdose, the disappearance of self during an orgasm, an ecstatic suicide? A fling off this precipice to fuse with the great mountain; to lie like one of the clutter of long trunk bodies of trees, scattered down the slope, lying as they fell and rolled, their stuff to be used again in a circular route through lichen, moss, fern, flower, tree, seed, chipmunk, weasel, hawk, and lichen?

I walked slowly past the tank to the end of the path. It stopped at the edge of a cliff. I sat hanging my feet over and tried to see what was below. An occasional thin place in the cloud revealed twinkling lights. I felt a train of sobs begin to rise inside. I swallowed hard, but they wouldn't be contained. I cried. Taught with humiliation since little that this was the sound of weakness, for once I let go. I thought it would never stop. Gasping, wet, disheveled, endless, racking crying—I had never known it. I couldn't catch my breath. For a moment I doubted—was this a show? But for what audience? Could I lie with breathless catches of my brain stem? I sat there for what seemed like hours, first crying, then laughing at my ludicrousness, then crying and laughing together.

On my way back I stopped at the tank. Hundreds of baby octopi were swimming around. At the bottom, shrunken into the little thing it likes to make of itself, the mother octopus was lying immobile. Had she decided to live? Was she dead?

I squeezed through. A dominant seventh chord, a leading tone, a fullness of the chest, a moment of insight, an early ray of the morning sun coming through the evergreen tops and caught in the grayish-pink clouds of a night-cooled mountain, the crunchy feeling of a fresh salad, the smell of newly wet pubic hair, the cracking sound of a new book, a wake-up siren, the smell of fresh coffee, the sound of silk panties sliding down across the knees, the discovery of the work of an artist who sees, the rush of mescaline, a footrace to the playground after hours of music practicing, an all-night jam session with a bass man and a drummer who throb with your brain, a sideways glance toward my groin by a passing pretty lady, a new idea about how a brain chemical works, flying conversations with unfettered brains, an escape from the repetitious dirge of the ageless musts of my middle brain. The amazement, the utter amazement that all of this could be mine. I got down on my knees in front of the tank to give thanks.

Attending Psychiatrist's Note: Patient found at 6:15 this morning in a utility closet off the solarium on the top floor of the hospital. The door leading to the roof was open. He was naked, on his knees on a blue blanket, crying and praying to a mop. When asked what he was doing, he said that a whole new life was waiting for him. It may have been a crisis of decision about suicide. He insisted on being called Dr. Sam Shambhala.

Kapilloff

TWELVE

"The trouble you bastards are having is that you aren't used to bargaining with the corpse. What do the firemen call it, the roast? It's a lot different than with relatives." Good eye gleaming, white teeth blazing against a deep Florida tan, my father was negotiating with the manager of Sarasota's most prestigious burial grounds. I went with him to the cemetery after being the guest artist in my mother's afternoon piano recital. It was my first trip from California after the episode with my heart. I gave a lecture-demonstration on the bebop harmonies of the fifties to her students and spoke about Thelonious Monk. Her proud smile brought back memories.

"Con-con, par-a-di-dle, stan-tee and con; con-con, par-a-didle, stan-tee and con." Sitting to the right of me daily on the piano bench, saying the rhythm in words, was the four-foot-eleven, blue-eyed, strong, and plain-faced woman who had given up her music school for over twenty years on the insistence of her husband. She cooked, kept a compulsively neat house, and had a music student population of one, me. Soft-spoken and reasonable in most other matters, in music she was an authoritarian pedagogue. Perfectionistic, she screamed and slapped. Sloppiness or inattention led to her biting her fingers, adding guilt to a student's fear. She demanded that each exercise have a harmonic analysis, correct fingering, the rhythm in words

147

(Con-stan-tee-no-ple; San Fran-cis-co; par-a-di-dle), and be played "with feeling." If her own infectious drive weren't enough and my daily 6:00 A.M. supervised practice didn't radiate cooperation, my father's half-shaved and angry face appeared around the corner. Bach's two- and three-part inventions, Czerny, Hanon, and the inverted scales in four octaves still give me a shaky excitement and nausea. Playing on taught me to charge rather than turn catatonic under pressure.

The mustached one was my first teacher of woodwinds. If I rushed home from school to practice the clarinet and saxophone, there would still be forty-five minutes left for the playground. Woodwind lessons were on Sunday and the dread mounted all week. A peculiar febrile illness often began on Friday afternoon; by Saturday I went to bed with unshakable drowsiness and diarrhea; on Sunday the lesson was canceled, the unconscious student-patient registering 102 degrees. At the age of twelve I got a new woodwind teacher—my father became the bogey man who would get me if I blew a cadenza. He drove me through a one-man saxophone recital at fourteen. I was to get a concerto, two sonatas, and four occasional pieces out of that jazz instrument without error. Working night and day during the last two weeks, my mouth bled as I played myself out of danger.

The survival theme in my music education prepared me well for any later lessons in modern social philosophy. The leaders of Western thought have taught us that life is a swim from rock to rock in dangerous waters; we breathe a sigh of relief when we make it. Darwin says that the weak will drown, leading to generations of stronger swimmers. Freud, aware of this selective process, theorized that the raw urges to swim, less adaptive on land but nonetheless present in high titer deep in the brain, get more hidden with socialization so the residual expressions of the swimming reflex must be deduced from Greek belly dancing, terminal seizures in the starved, and intercourse in the missionary posture. Marx suggested that getting safely to rocks, once tied to survival, has become symbolic—at every level of society, commerce in rocks has become the major determinant of social organization. Lord Keynes said that the government could make rocks out of plastic and manufacture a stable economy and redistribute safety more fairly. Was there any energy left for nonsurvival things like art? Erikson peeled a few rocks loose that were too little to hang onto and arranged them in decorative patterns. The neo-Freudian psychoanalysts, acknowledging the disappearing role of drowning in the creation of the final shape of man—now that the government has jammed the water with plastic rocks and search-and-rescue teams— still talk about *cultural* selection. It's all in the language of fear and middle-brain red. My mother's and father's *mama-loshen*.

I had arrived the evening before the recital and my father whispered that he had a secret to share at the cemetery. He is a healthy seventy-six, having beaten retinal cancer, the arteriosclerotic loss of circulation to his legs, and the usual atrophy of the self. A cemetery didn't make sense.

"Your father is something else. We haven't seen anything like him." Stomach-popping buttons over wrinkled seersucker slacks, the straw-chewing mortuary owner was fascinated. "He comes out here about every week, looks things over, haggles about price, and then leaves. He always tells one of his funny Jewish stories. Real shrewd. He says he's been waiting on you to make the final decision."

Playing in my mother's recital and helping my father bury himself made for quite an afternoon. I blamed the Florida sun and humidity for my feeling of faintness.

My father and I walked among the graves. "I've given it a lot of thought. There're a number of things to be considered. I want to be in a place that will let me see the sun in the morning. You know how much I like it. So my first thought was over there." He pointed to a small elevation with an unimpeded eastern view. "On the other hand, out in the open I can get rained on. You know what Florida rain is like, with no warning. So my next thought was over here." We walked to a large building with crypts lining the outside walls. "I could still see the sun and the building would protect me from flash floods." My head began to hum.

"But then I thought of the body snatchers."

"The what?!"

"The body snatchers. When I was a little boy in Baltimore, we lived in the slums near the Johns Hopkins Medical School. Every year, families that needed money went out at night and dug up bodies for the medical students to cut up. Once the five dollars I got for a skull bought groceries for a week. You could use a screwdriver and pry this little lock open and I'd be gone."

"As you probably know, Dad, they don't do that kind of thing anymore. There're plenty of bodies that have either been willed or are unclaimed. There are laws that . . ."

"Yes, yes, I know all that. Sarasota is growing and there's going to be a medical school here someday. I don't want to take a chance. So it's come down to this place." We walked to a small blue mosque, lined on three sides with crypts facing in, a large and ornate metal gate closing off the fourth. A thick, blue all-weather rug, two small white marble benches, and an elaborate blue and white chandelier made up the internal appointments. "If I choose the two on the wall opposite the gate, I'd still be able to see the morning sun, be under roof and off the ground, and the locked gate would protect me from the body snatchers. What do you think?"

"It seems to me you've hit upon a perfect compromise." My mouth was almost too dry to talk.

"Both your mother and I will lie sideways. Her feet won't be in my face, and mine won't be in hers. Also, this way," he looked at me from under his waxed, black, bushy eyebrows with a wink, "she can knock if she needs me.

"You'll have a key. You'll come and we'll talk." We

left the mosque and walked toward the car along a path that passed a regal regiment of birds of paradise and under a large oak with a gray, frizzy beard of Spanish moss. It was hot and my shirt was wet.

"If you approve, I'll close the deal. They've come down several thousand dollars. I'm waiting for them to get hungrier."

"It looks good to me."

"Oh, yes, I forgot to add . . . we're going to have those self-sealing caskets. You'll be able to dig me up in two hundred years and I'll be just the same." His smile was beautiful.

He suggested that we sit together before we left the park and I was grateful. We found a place on a carpet of Bermuda grass under an oak where the shade cooled the warm breeze. We sat cross-legged, facing each other.

"You know my secret and now you'll have to tell me yours."

"What do you mean? I don't have any secrets."

"You must have." He was serious.

"I don't know what you're talking about."

"What would you say if a forty-two-year-old son of yours had done what you have?"

"What's that?"

"You worked your ass off going through medical school, residency, and research training on your own, after I cut you off financially. You made a long marriage with a beautiful and brilliant girl, and you together had two handsome and smart sons. You became the youngest professor and chairman of a psychiatry department in America. She became a famous psychologist. You've written two hundred scientific papers and five books, most of the names I can't even pronounce. I've lost track of your consultantships, editorships, grants, lectures, and the rest of it. You're a distinguished physician and scientist."

"You sound like my grandmother."

"Wait. I'm not finished. You made it. Do you know

what that means? I had to leave school at the age of eight to carry shopping bags, and my son is all these things. *We* made it!"

"I don't know what you're driving at."

"Shut up till I'm finished." His voice was quiet but his real brown eye flashed. There was still a lot of fire left. "Then you started the crazy stuff. Hung out with a professional football team and got in trouble in all the newspapers. You're going to be crucified for that football book. I told you not to publish it. You walked out of your marriage after twenty-two years. Your oldest boy ran away to Europe before he finished college. You resigned your chairmanship and grew long hair. You don't wear a tie and talk funny. I read Alan Watts too, but that far-out shit you're writing . . . you can't get people's respect. The last one you sent me about that octopus, now that's a *real* crazy book. And what's more, you stole it."

"I what?"

"You stole the whole idea, the book, the whole thing. From Gogol."

"Dad, please, this once, leave my new . . . I . . ."

"No, wait, you should know. Gogol wrote a thing about a madman and put a bunch of real stuff in there and then he put a talking dog. So you put a talking octopus. Gogol has high-flown and fancy right next to low-down and dirty, and you have the blue-white color of awe with fucking in a phone booth and a penis for car radios. Next you'll steal Gogol's guy without a nose."

"Dad, I really don't think . . ."

"Most of all, it's so stupid to have to tell everybody your problems. What's wrong with you anyway? Are you really sick? I mean, other people leave their wives without writing a crazy book. Do you need another analysis? I'll even pay for it. Is it drugs? Is it a woman? What the hell could have done this to you? What are you doing? For God's sake, what are you doing?" He was shouting. I used to think his fear was anger.

"Do you want the truth?" I made myself firm.

"Of course I want the truth!"

"The truth is, I don't know. And for the first time in my life, I'm not going to make anything up." Sitting cross-legged in the grass in my white muslin pants and long wet shirt, I was a stubborn Gandhi talking to the administrators. "So at least tell me, who's this Dr. Sam Shambhala you turned into? The name isn't even Jewish. Do you think people are going to send you patients after reading that kind of stuff—praying to a mop!"

"It took me a little while to remember where that name came from. I must have gotten it from that guy in Berkeley who puts out the *Tibetan Book of the Dead*."

"What kind of a name for a book is that, *Tibetan Book of the Dead*? Are you going to call your book *Dr. Sam Shambhala and the Octopus*? If you, in your present condition, still remember a little basic Yiddish, you should pardon me, but I think you should call the book *Dr. Schlim Schlimazel and the Oy Vays.* What do you need it for? Why make yourself trouble? Enjoy! Take what you've earned."

"Ah. That's what the struggle is about, to stop the struggle. It's only lately that I found out that struggling won't do it. It's the reverse. What works is to surrender. To detach. The personality of Buddhism, a renunciation, rather than the affirmation of something like Hinduism, is the way that fits. I tend to be a little rebellious. As Bubba Free John says . . ."

"Wait! You're telling me that there's a Jewish grandmother that calls herself Free John? Already it's too much. It's too much already!"

He was silent for several minutes as he stared at the ground. I waited. His face gradually relaxed. "Arnold, I don't know how to say these things to you because we talk so different, but what *real* things have you found? I mean besides all the fancy words." He was suddenly not challenging but curious. The histrionics were gone.

"I think you'll laugh at what I've found so far. It

sounds so corny. So far, I know that it feels good to run
for a long time; that lying in bed is not on nervous nails
but something soft and warm; listening to Ross talk about
his life with his friends is a window into magic rather than
a sample of his social skills at work, to be evaluated, fixed;
that quiet is rich and full and not loneliness; that a wild
flower has, besides a name, some beautiful colors. All I've
found so far is what you would call little stuff. I've wondered if that's all there is—which by the way is much more
than I had." I saw my father nod his head in agreement!

"You fancy professors sure take the long way around.
Don't you remember that after I got cancer and almost
died, I worked like hell to pile up enough money for us
to make it, and then I came to Sarasota to walk on the
beach? I was only forty-eight, and my CPA said that in a
few years I would be a very wealthy man; he thought that
my quitting was a sign of craziness. Do you know what I
do when I walk on the beach, two hours every morning?
I recite the Hebrew alphabet backwards. Over and over.
I started it by accident twenty-five years ago, and I discovered that it emptied out my mind. Pretty soon the Gulf
of Mexico began to sparkle. I felt light enough to fly. The
money and my business got distant and unimportant.
Even you going three thousand miles away to college and
not coming home much, which almost killed your mother,
didn't hurt as much as I expected. I found myself going
with the tide—not forcing anything. Then I made another
discovery. Before dinner, every day, I play the clarinet. If
I hold tones in the lower register for a long time, I feel
the vibrations in my head. If I do that for thirty minutes,
funny things happen. First my mind gets quiet and then
thoughts begin about time, beauty, death, and most of all
God. My God, not anyone else's. He comes to me and
talks quietly when He thinks it's necessary. Usually when
I'm on the beach or when I'm playing the clarinet. I can
hear His voice. He tells me that things will take care of
themselves. He's even taken away that temper of mine,

except once in a great while when that mother of yours pushes one of my buttons, and I don't have many left."

I was stunned. My suspiciousness made me search his face for evidence of a game—a satire, a lesson by caricature. "Why haven't you told me? I mean, you've never spoken once about any of this." His warm smile was a new sight. His eye twinkled.

"If you had a big-mogul psychiatrist son would you tell him about hearing voices? I mean, your contempt for me was enough. After I read your octopus book I knew that your journey had begun. It was a little earlier than mine, but so was your cancer and heart trouble. I wonder if you're going to leave psychiatry like I left my business. I had to challenge you—to see if it was all just rebellion. When you didn't get defensive I began to believe."

I felt the tears begin behind my eyes, my nose fill up. I had thought it would take years to get unstuck.

We didn't speak again as we walked to his midnight blue Lincoln Continental with the open sunroof. As we drove out of the cemetery he couldn't resist. "There's only one thing. Maybe if you didn't make so much noise about it, your trip would be easier." He looked over at me with his new smile. "What do you think?"

ABOUT THE AUTHOR

Arnold J. Mandell, M.D., is a Professor of Psychiatry, Neurosciences, Physiology and Pharmacology at the University of California Medical School at San Diego, where he is cochairman of the Department of Psychiatry. Mandell graduated magna cum laude and Phi Beta Kappa from Stanford University and attended medical school at Tulane University. He did his residency at the University of California at Los Angeles. He is a member of eighteen professional societies, including the American Psychiatric Association and the American Academy of Psychoanalysis. He is the recipient of numerous research grants, including four from the National Institute of Mental Health, and was the first person to address the plenary sessions of both the American Academy of Psychoanalysis and the Society of Biological Psychiatry, and he did so on the same day, May 1, 1977. He is the editor of four books in his field and the author of *The Nightmare Season* and of 200 original articles in the brain sciences. He won the Pushcart Prize for an essay originally published in *The Ontario Review*.